HOLLY JOLLY COOKIES & CAKES

100+ Delicious Treats for the Most Wonderful Time of the Year

ALEXIS MERSEL

CENTENNIAL BOOKS

CANDY CANE
LAYER CAKE,
PAGE 75

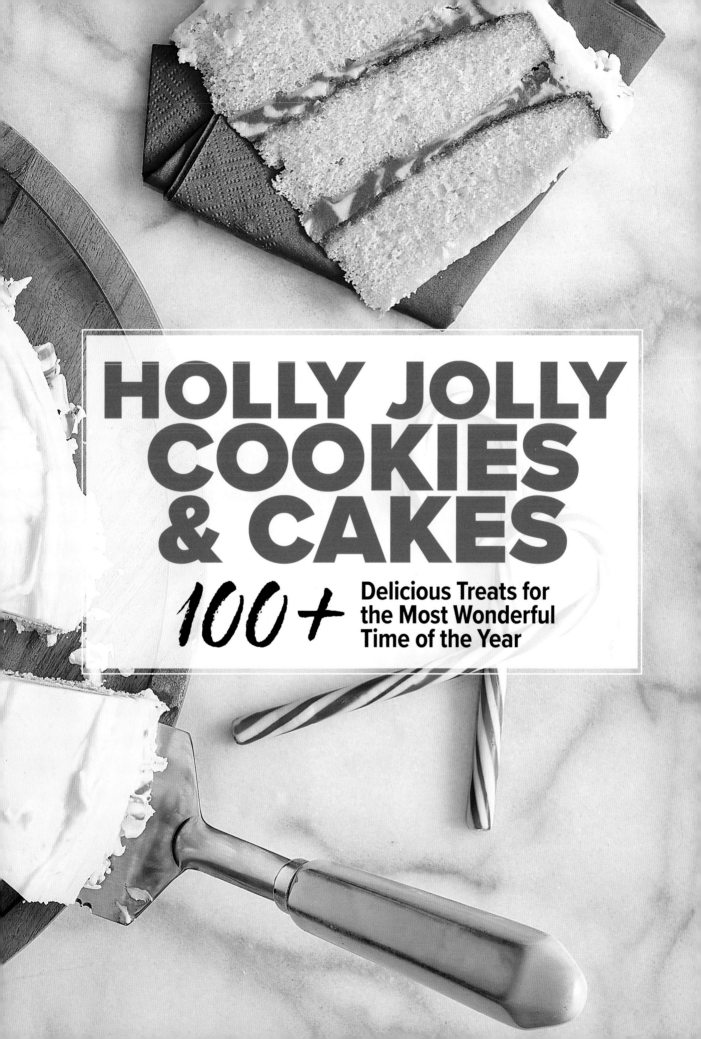

HOLLY JOLLY COOKIES & CAKES

100+

Delicious Treats for the Most Wonderful Time of the Year

SPREAD HOLIDAY CHEER WITH SWEET TREATS!

As soon as you reach for a cozy sweater to greet the first frost or snuggle up under a blanket with a piping hot mug of hot chocolate, it can only mean one thing—holiday baking season is here! For many of us, it's the most wonderful time of the year. The magic of colored sprinkles, the first bite of a chewy gingerbread cookie, the sweet swirls of frosting atop a holiday spice cake—no winter would be complete without a stunning array of festive goodies.

At the heart of every holiday season is a kitchen filled with the aromas of freshly baked cookies. Choose from easy drop cookies, fancy cutouts, mouthwatering bars or showstopping specialty confections—all baked in batches big enough to feed a crowd. We've filled this book with loads of recipes that you can prep in advance and decorate in countless ways.

Oh, and we'd be remiss not to mention the oodles of cakes that make this season even more delicious, including dazzling layer confections, flavor-packed bundts, anytime quick breads, cute cupcakes and specialty cakes that will be sure to impress guests. You'll be surprised how easy it is to transform timeless recipes into holiday-worthy desserts with a few festive flavors. From classics to the unexpected, we have something for everyone.

We hope you'll find a new seasonal favorite, and use our tips to perfect your go-to staples, among the countless treats here for giving (and keeping). 'Tis the season to bake with abandon.

Happy Holidays!

ALEXIS MERSEL

6

94

58

112

66

48

Contents

SUGAR & SPICE
MOLASSES CRINKLES,
PAGE 9

Chapter 1

Drop Cookies

BAKE A BIG BATCH OF THESE COOKIE SWAP–WORTHY
TREATS, FROM CLASSIC CHOCOLATE CRACKLES
TO FESTIVE PEANUT BUTTER KISSES COVERED
IN CHRISTMAS-COLORED SPRINKLES.

**OATMEAL,
WHITE CHOCOLATE
& CRANBERRY
COOKIES**

Sugar & Spice Molasses Crinkles

Easy • Make Ahead • Nut-Free

A few drops of water will give these cookies their crackled look. Using an eye dropper makes this step easy—and fun.

PREP 20 minutes
CHILL 1 hour or up to overnight
BAKE 10 minutes per batch
MAKES 4 dozen cookies

INGREDIENTS

- 4½ cups all-purpose flour
- 4 teaspoons baking soda
- 2 teaspoons ground cinnamon
- 2 teaspoons ground ginger
- 1 teaspoon ground cloves
- 1 teaspoon kosher salt
- 1½ cups shortening, softened (such as Crisco)
- 2 cups firmly packed dark brown sugar
- 2 large eggs, lightly beaten
- ½ cup unsulfured blackstrap molasses
- ½ cup granulated sugar

INSTRUCTIONS

1. In a medium bowl, whisk together flour, baking soda, cinnamon, ginger, cloves and salt.
2. In a large bowl, using a wooden spoon, mix together shortening, brown sugar, eggs and molasses. Add flour mixture and mix with a spoon or your hands until the dough comes together. Flatten dough into a disk, divide into 3 pieces, cover each tightly with plastic wrap, and refrigerate until firm, for at least 1 hour or up to overnight.
3. Preheat oven to 350°F. Line 2 baking sheets with parchment paper.
4. Place granulated sugar in a small bowl. Working 1 piece at a time, scoop rounded tablespoons of dough (or use an ice cream scoop 1½ inches in diameter) into the palms of your hands and roll into balls. Roll each ball in granulated sugar. Place balls 2 inches apart on prepared baking sheets, then use the tips of your fingers to gently flatten each ball into a ¾-inch-thick round. Dip both sides of the dough round in sugar again. Using a small spoon or eye dropper, sprinkle each round with 2 to 3 very small drops of water (this will give the cookies a crackled surface). Bake, one sheet at a time, 10 minutes or until surfaces crack. Cool on baking sheets 5 minutes. Sprinkle with more sugar, if desired. Transfer cookies to wire cooling racks to cool completely.
NOTE You can prepare the dough a day ahead and bake the cookies whenever you like, or bake them in separate batches.

Oatmeal, White Chocolate & Cranberry Cookies

Easy • Family Favorite • Nut-Free

The tartness of dried cranberries balances the sweetness of white chocolate, while old-fashioned rolled oats add a chewy texture to the mix.

PREP 20 minutes
BAKE 12 to 14 minutes per batch
MAKES 3½ dozen cookies

INGREDIENTS

- 1½ cups all-purpose flour
- 1 teaspoon baking soda
- ½ teaspoon kosher salt
- 1 cup (2 sticks) unsalted butter, at room temperature
- ¾ cup granulated sugar
- ¾ cup firmly packed light brown sugar
- 1 large egg
- 1 teaspoon vanilla extract
- 2 cups old-fashioned rolled oats (not quick cooking)
- 1 cup white chocolate chips
- 1 cup dried cranberries

INSTRUCTIONS

1. Preheat oven to 350°F. Line 3 baking sheets with parchment paper. Set aside.
2. In a medium bowl, whisk together flour, baking soda and salt.
3. In a large bowl, using an electric mixer, beat butter and both sugars together on medium-high speed until pale and fluffy, about 2 minutes. Scrape down the sides of the bowl with a rubber spatula. Add egg and vanilla and beat on medium-high speed until well combined. Scrape down the sides of the bowl. Add flour mixture and beat on low speed just until combined. Using a rubber spatula, stir in oats, white chocolate and cranberries.
4. Drop dough by rounded tablespoons (or use an ice cream scoop 1½ inches in diameter) 2 inches apart onto prepared baking sheets. Bake, one sheet at a time, 12 to 14 minutes or until set and golden brown. Cool on baking sheets 1 to 2 minutes. Transfer cookies to wire cooling racks to cool completely.

quick tip

Oatmeal cookies are a blank slate for a variety of mix-ins—try dried fruit like cherries or currants, nuts like pecans or walnuts and/or sweets like cinnamon or dark chocolate chips.

Butterscotch-Toasted Coconut Cookies

Easy • Nut-Free

Try white, milk or dark chocolate chips instead of butterscotch chips for a tasty variation.

PREP 15 minutes
BAKE 14 minutes per batch
MAKES 2 dozen cookies

INGREDIENTS

- 1 **cup sweetened shredded coconut**
- 1⅓ **cups all-purpose flour**
- ½ **teaspoon baking powder**
- ½ **teaspoon baking soda**
- ½ **teaspoon kosher salt**
- ½ **cup (1 stick) unsalted butter, at room temperature**
- ½ **cup granulated sugar**
- ½ **cup firmly packed light brown sugar**
- 1 **large egg**
- 1 **teaspoon vanilla extract**
- 1 **cup butterscotch chips**

INSTRUCTIONS

1. Preheat oven to 325°F. Line 2 baking sheets with parchment paper. Spread coconut evenly across one of the prepared baking sheets and toast until very light brown, 3 to 4 minutes. (Keep a close eye on coconut so that it doesn't burn.) Cool on a wire rack while you make the dough.

2. In a medium bowl, whisk together flour, baking powder, baking soda and salt.

3. In a large bowl, using an electric mixer, beat butter and both sugars together on medium-high speed until pale and fluffy, about 2 minutes. Add egg and vanilla and beat on medium-high speed until well combined. Using a rubber spatula, scrape down the sides of the bowl. Add flour mixture and beat on low speed just until combined. Stir in toasted coconut and butterscotch chips with the rubber spatula.

4. Drop dough by rounded tablespoons (or use an ice cream scoop 1½ inches in diameter) about 2 inches apart onto the prepared baking sheets. Bake, one sheet at a time, 14 to 15 minutes or until cookies are set and golden brown. Cool on baking sheets 5 minutes. Transfer cookies to wire cooling racks to cool completely.

Jam Thumbprints

Classic • Family Favorite
Nut-Free

Use an assortment of your favorite jams in these cookies. To shape the center, a thumbprint looks rustic, while a teaspoon gives a polished look—both are great options.

PREP 25 minutes
CHILL 30 minutes
BAKE 12 to 13 minutes per batch
MAKES 2½ dozen cookies

INGREDIENTS

- 2 cups all-purpose flour, plus more for dusting
- ½ teaspoon kosher salt
- 1 cup (2 sticks) unsalted butter, at room temperature
- ¾ cup sugar
- 1 teaspoon vanilla extract
- 1 cup raspberry, strawberry or apricot jam, or a combination

INSTRUCTIONS

1. In a medium bowl, whisk together flour and salt.

2. In a large bowl, using an electric mixer, beat butter and sugar together on medium-high speed until pale and fluffy, about 2 minutes. Scrape down the sides of the bowl with a rubber spatula. Add vanilla and beat on medium speed until well combined. Add flour mixture and beat on low speed just until combined and dough starts to come together.

3. Lightly dust a clean work surface with flour. Scrape the dough onto the work surface and shape into a disk. Cover tightly with plastic wrap and refrigerate for 30 minutes.

4. Preheat oven to 350°F. Line 3 baking sheets with parchment paper.

5. Remove the dough from the refrigerator, scoop rounded tablespoons of dough into the palms of your hands and roll into balls. Place balls 2 inches apart on prepared baking sheets. Using your thumb or the back of a teaspoon measuring spoon, make an indentation in the center of each cookie. Bake, one sheet at a time, 8 minutes or until just starting to set. Remove the sheet from the oven and fill each indentation with ½ teaspoon jam. (If the cookies have puffed up, use the teaspoon to indent the centers again.) Return sheet to oven and bake until jam is set, 4–5 minutes longer. Cool on baking sheets 5 minutes. Transfer cookies to wire cooling racks to cool completely.

quick tip

To keep your brown sugar from hardening while in your pantry, add a marshmallow or two to the bag.

Dark Chocolate-Rye Cookies With Sea Salt

Family Favorite • Nut-Free

Sprinkling these rich cookies with flaky sea salt, such as Maldon, just before baking intensifies the flavor of the chocolate.

PREP	20 minutes
CHILL	30 minutes to 1 hour
BAKE	8 to 10 minutes per batch
MAKES	2 dozen cookies

INGREDIENTS

- 4 tablespoons (½ stick) unsalted butter, cut into pieces
- 12 ounces bittersweet chocolate, coarsely chopped
- ¾ cup rye flour
- ¼ cup all-purpose flour
- 1 teaspoon baking powder
- ½ teaspoon kosher salt
- 1 cup firmly packed dark brown sugar
- 3 large eggs
- 1 tablespoon unsulfured molasses
- 2 teaspoons vanilla extract
- Flaky sea salt, for sprinkling

INSTRUCTIONS

1. Set a medium saucepan on the stovetop over low heat. Add butter and chocolate and stir constantly with a rubber spatula until the butter and chocolate have melted and the mixture is smooth, about 4 minutes. Remove pan from heat and let cool for 10 minutes.

2. Meanwhile, in a small bowl, whisk together the flours, baking powder and salt.

3. In a large bowl, using an electric mixer, beat sugar and eggs on medium-high speed until smooth and slightly thickened, about 3 minutes. Add cooled chocolate mixture, molasses and vanilla and beat until blended and shiny, 1 minute. Scrape down the sides of the bowl with a rubber spatula. Add flour mixture and beat on low speed just until combined. Cover the bowl with plastic wrap and refrigerate for 30 minutes to 1 hour, or until dough is slightly firm.

4. Preheat oven to 350°F. Line 2 baking sheets with parchment paper.

5. Drop dough by rounded tablespoons (or use an ice cream scoop 1½ inches in diameter) 2 inches apart onto prepared baking sheets. Sprinkle with sea salt and bake, one sheet at a time, 8 to 10 minutes or until the cookies are puffed and starting to crack. Cool on baking sheets 1 to 2 minutes. Transfer cookies to wire cooling racks to cool completely.

Citrus-Poppy Seed Thins
Classic • Easy

Invest in a microplane to make zesting citrus fruits a breeze. Most cost around $15.

PREP 30 minutes
BAKE 12 to 13 minutes per batch
MAKES 2½ dozen cookies

INGREDIENTS

Finely grated zest and juice from 1 large lemon (about 1½ teaspoons zest and ¼ cup juice)

1 cup (2 sticks) unsalted butter, at room temperature, divided

2 cups all-purpose flour

1 tablespoon poppy seeds, plus more for sprinkling

1 teaspoon baking powder

½ teaspoon kosher salt

1¼ cups sugar, plus 3 tablespoons for shaping cookies

1 large egg

1½ teaspoons vanilla extract
Finely grated zest from 1 lime (about 1 teaspoon)

INSTRUCTIONS

1. In a small saucepan set on the stovetop over medium heat, add lemon juice and bring to a simmer. Cook until reduced by half. Add 1 stick butter and cook until melted. Remove from the heat and set aside to cool for 10 minutes.

2. Preheat oven to 350°F. Line 3 baking sheets with parchment paper. Set aside.

3. In a medium bowl, whisk together flour, 1 tablespoon poppy seeds, baking powder and salt.

4. In a large bowl, using an electric mixer, beat the remaining 1 stick butter and the 1¼ cups sugar together on medium-high speed until pale and fluffy, about 2 minutes. Scrape down the sides of the bowl with a rubber spatula. Add egg and reserved lemon butter and beat until creamy, about 1 minute. Add vanilla, lemon and lime zests and beat on medium-high speed until well combined. Scrape down the sides of the bowl. Add flour mixture and beat on low speed just until combined. Dough will be soft.

5. Place remaining 3 tablespoons sugar in a small shallow bowl.

6. Drop dough by rounded tablespoons (or use an ice cream scoop 1½ inches in diameter) 2 inches apart onto prepared baking sheets. Dip the bottom of a glass in sugar and press each ball into a ¼-inch-thick round about 3 inches in diameter. Sprinkle with poppy seeds. Bake, one sheet at a time, 12 to 13 minutes or until edges are golden brown. Let cool completely on baking sheets.

Chocolate Chip-Walnut Cookies

Easy • Family Favorite
Make Ahead

A small amount of water helps bind the cookie dough together, making it easy to shape into balls. You can omit the walnuts if you prefer a nut-free cookie.

PREP	20 minutes
CHILL	30 minutes or up to 2 days
BAKE	9 to 10 minutes per batch
MAKES	3½ dozen cookies

INGREDIENTS

- 2¼ cups all-purpose flour
- 1 teaspoon baking soda
- 1 teaspoon kosher salt
- 1 cup (2 sticks) unsalted butter, at room temperature
- 1 cup firmly packed dark brown sugar
- ½ cup granulated sugar
- 2 large eggs
- 1 teaspoon vanilla extract
- 1 (12 ounce) bag semisweet chocolate chips
- 1 cup chopped walnuts (optional)
- 1 teaspoon cold water

INSTRUCTIONS

1. In a medium bowl, whisk together flour, baking soda and salt.

2. In a large bowl, using an electric mixer, beat butter and both sugars together on medium-high speed until light and fluffy, about 2 minutes. Scrape down the sides of the bowl with a rubber spatula. Add eggs and vanilla and beat just until combined. Add flour mixture and beat on low speed just until combined, about 30 seconds. Using a rubber spatula or wooden spoon, stir in chocolate chips, nuts (if using) and water. Flatten dough into a disk, cover tightly with plastic wrap, and refrigerate for at least 30 minutes or up to 2 days.

3. Preheat oven to 350°F. Line 3 baking sheets with parchment paper.

4. Scoop rounded tablespoons of dough (or use an ice cream scoop 1½ inches in diameter) into the palms of your hands and roll into balls. Place balls 2 inches apart on prepared baking sheets. Bake, one sheet at a time, 9 to 10 minutes or until browned around the edges. Cool on baking sheets 5 minutes. Transfer cookies to wire cooling racks to cool completely.

NOTE This dough is best refrigerated overnight, but you can wait up to 2 days to bake the cookies, or make a small batch each night.

Gluten-Free Chocolate-Almond Cookies

Easy • Family Favorite

Add 1 cup of bittersweet, semisweet or white chocolate chips to these soft and chewy cookies for an extra punch of chocolate.

PREP 15 minutes
CHILL 30 minutes
BAKE 10 to 12 minutes per batch
MAKES 2 dozen cookies

INGREDIENTS

- 1½ cups almond flour
- ½ cup unsweetened cocoa powder
- 1½ teaspoons baking powder
- ½ teaspoon kosher salt
- ½ cup (1 stick) unsalted butter, at room temperature
- ⅔ cup granulated sugar
- ⅓ cup firmly packed light brown sugar
- 2 large eggs
- ½ teaspoon vanilla extract
- ¼ teaspoon almond extract
- 1 cup semisweet, bittersweet or white chocolate chips (optional)

INSTRUCTIONS

1. In a medium bowl, whisk together flour, cocoa powder, baking powder and salt.

2. In a large bowl, using an electric mixer, beat butter and both sugars together on medium speed until light and fluffy, about 2 minutes. Scrape down the sides of the bowl with a rubber spatula. Add eggs, vanilla and almond extracts and beat until well combined. Scrape down the sides of the bowl. Add flour mixture and beat on low speed just until combined. Using a rubber spatula, stir in chocolate chips, if using. Cover the bowl with plastic wrap and refrigerate for 30 minutes.

3. Preheat oven to 350°F. Line 2 baking sheets with parchment paper.

4. Drop dough by rounded tablespoons (or use an ice cream scoop 1½ inches in diameter) 2 inches apart onto prepared baking sheets. Bake, one sheet at a time, 10 to 12 minutes or until cookies are puffed and tops start to crackle. Cool on baking sheets 5 minutes. Transfer cookies to wire cooling racks to cool completely.

quick tip

Don't confuse almond meal with almond flour. Meal is more coarse. Finely-ground almond flour is best for baking.

PEANUT BUTTER KISSES

Peanut Butter Kisses
Classic • Easy • Family Favorite

*The festive sprinkles add
a holiday touch to these
classic peanut butter cookies.*

PREP 20 minutes
CHILL 1 hour
BAKE 8 minutes per batch
MAKES 2 dozen cookies

INGREDIENTS

- 1¼ cups all-purpose flour
- ½ teaspoon baking soda
- ½ teaspoon baking powder
- ½ teaspoon kosher salt
- ½ cup (1 stick) unsalted butter, at room temperature
- ¾ cup creamy peanut butter
- ½ cup granulated sugar
- ½ cup firmly packed light brown sugar
- 1 large egg
- 1 teaspoon vanilla extract
- ¾ cup nonpareil sprinkles
- 24 chocolate kiss candies, wrappers removed

INSTRUCTIONS

1. In a medium bowl, whisk together flour, baking soda, baking powder and salt.

2. In a large bowl, using an electric mixer, beat butter, peanut butter and both sugars together on medium-high speed until smooth and fluffy, about 2 minutes. Scrape down the sides of the bowl with a rubber spatula. Add egg and vanilla and beat on medium-high speed until well combined. Scrape down the sides of the bowl. Add flour mixture and beat on low speed just until combined. Cover the bowl with plastic wrap and refrigerate until firm, about 1 hour.

3. Preheat oven to 375°F. Line 2 baking sheets with parchment paper.

4. Place sprinkles in a small bowl.

5. Scoop rounded tablespoons of dough (or use an ice cream scoop 1½ inches in diameter) into the palms of your hands and roll into balls. Roll each ball in sprinkles, pressing gently to adhere. Place balls 2 inches apart on prepared baking sheets. Bake, one sheet at a time, 8 minutes or until lightly browned and puffed. Let cool 1 minute, then lightly press a chocolate kiss into the center of each cookie. Cool on baking sheets 5 minutes. Transfer cookies to wire cooling racks to cool completely.

Soft & Chewy Gingerbread Cookies
Easy • Family Favorite • Nut-Free

*These beloved holiday treats come
together in minutes and fill
your kitchen with the irresistible
aromas of the season.*

PREP 15 minutes
BAKE 10 minutes per batch
MAKES 2 dozen cookies

INGREDIENTS

- 2 cups all-purpose flour
- 1½ teaspoons baking soda
- ½ teaspoon kosher salt
- 2 teaspoons ground ginger
- 2 teaspoons ground cinnamon
- ½ teaspoon ground nutmeg
- ½ teaspoon ground cloves
- ½ cup (1 stick) unsalted butter, at room temperature
- ¾ cup firmly packed light brown sugar
- 1 large egg
- ½ cup molasses

quick tip
Add chocolate kisses
one minute after baking,
so they set but
don't melt.

INSTRUCTIONS

1. Preheat oven to 350°F. Line 2 baking sheets with parchment paper. Set aside.

2. In a medium bowl, whisk together flour, baking soda, salt, ginger, cinnamon, nutmeg and cloves.

3. In a large bowl, using an electric mixer, beat butter and sugar on medium-high speed until light and fluffy, about 2 minutes. Scrape down the sides of the bowl with a rubber spatula. Add egg and beat until combined. Add molasses and beat until smooth, about 1 minute. Scrape down the sides of the bowl. Add flour mixture and beat on low speed just until combined, 30 seconds.

4. Drop dough by rounded tablespoons (or use an ice cream scoop 1½ inches in diameter) 2 inches apart onto prepared baking sheets. Bake, one sheet at a time, for 10 minutes or until set and starting to crack. Cool on baking sheets 1 to 2 minutes. Transfer cookies to wire cooling racks to cool completely.

Lemon-Cornmeal-Currant Cookies

Easy • Nut-Free

Rehydrating dried currants intensifies their flavor and improves their texture. You can swap them for dried cranberries or leave the dried fruit out entirely.

PREP 15 minutes

BAKE 14 to 15 minutes per batch

MAKES 2 dozen cookies

INGREDIENTS

- ½ cup dried currants
- 1½ cups all-purpose flour
- 1 cup cornmeal
- ½ teaspoon kosher salt
- 1½ sticks unsalted butter, at room temperature
- 1 cup sugar, plus more for sprinkling
- 1 large egg
- 2 teaspoons finely grated lemon zest (from 1 large lemon)

INSTRUCTIONS

1. Preheat oven to 350°F. Line 2 baking sheets with parchment paper. Set aside.

2. Place the currants in a small heatproof bowl and cover with very hot tap water. Let them soak while you prepare the cookie dough.

3. In a medium bowl, whisk together flour, cornmeal and salt.

4. In a large bowl, using an electric mixer, beat butter and sugar together on medium-high speed until pale and fluffy, about 2 minutes. Scrape down the sides of the bowl with a rubber spatula. Add egg and lemon zest and beat until creamy, about 1 minute. Scrape down the sides of the bowl. Add the flour mixture and beat on low speed just until combined and the dough starts to come together.

5. Drain the currants and place them on a paper towel–lined plate. Pat dry. Using a rubber spatula, stir currants into the dough.

6. Drop dough by rounded tablespoons (or use an ice cream scoop 1½ inches in diameter) 2 inches apart onto prepared baking sheets. Sprinkle with sugar and use the bottom of a glass or your fingers to flatten balls to ¾-inch thickness. Bake, one sheet at a time, 14 to 15 minutes or until lightly browned around the edges. Cool on baking sheets 1 to 2 minutes. Transfer cookies to wire cooling racks to cool completely.

quick tip

Using unsalted butter allows you to control the exact amount of salt in your batter.

Double Chocolate Cookies
Family Favorite • Nut-Free

These one-bowl treats taste just like brownies. Use a bread knife to chop chocolate and include any stray chocolate shards in the dough, too.

PREP 25 minutes
CHILL 10 minutes
BAKE 10 minutes per batch
MAKES 2 dozen cookies

INGREDIENTS

- 4 tablespoons (½ stick) unsalted butter, cut into pieces
- 8 ounces semisweet or bittersweet chocolate, chopped, plus 4 ounces cut into 1-inch chunks
- ¾ cup all-purpose flour
- ½ teaspoon baking powder
- ½ teaspoon kosher salt
- ¾ cup firmly packed light brown sugar
- 2 large eggs
- 1 teaspoon vanilla extract

INSTRUCTIONS

1. Preheat oven to 350°F. Line 2 baking sheets with parchment paper. Set aside.
2. Set a medium saucepan on the stovetop over low heat. Add butter and the 8 ounces chopped chocolate and stir constantly with a rubber spatula until the butter and chocolate have melted and the mixture is smooth. Remove saucepan from heat and let cool for 10 minutes.
3. Meanwhile, in a small bowl, whisk together flour, baking powder and salt.
4. Add sugar, eggs and vanilla to chocolate mixture and stir until blended. Whisk in flour mixture. Using a rubber spatula, fold in the remaining 4 ounces chocolate chunks. Cover the saucepan with plastic wrap and refrigerate for 10 minutes.
5. Drop dough by rounded tablespoons (or use an ice cream scoop 1½ inches in diameter) 2 inches apart onto prepared baking sheets. Return dough to refrigerator between batches. Bake, one sheet at a time, 10 minutes or until the edges are set but the centers are still soft. Cool on baking sheets 1 to 2 minutes. Transfer cookies to wire cooling racks to cool completely.

½ cup (1 stick) unsalted butter, at room temperature
½ cup granulated sugar
½ cup firmly packed light brown sugar
2 large eggs
1 teaspoon vanilla extract
1 cup creamy peanut butter
Peanut Butter Filling (page 124)

INSTRUCTIONS

1. In a medium bowl, whisk flour, baking powder, baking soda and salt.

2. In a large bowl, using an electric mixer, beat butter and both sugars together on medium-high speed until light and fluffy, about 2 minutes. Scrape down the sides of the bowl with a rubber spatula. Add eggs and vanilla and beat well until combined, 1 minute. Add peanut butter and beat until combined. Scrape down the sides of the bowl. Add flour mixture and beat on low speed until just combined, 1 minute. Cover the bowl tightly with plastic wrap and refrigerate until the dough is firm enough to scoop and no longer sticky, about 2 hours.

3. Preheat oven to 350°F. Line 3 baking sheets with parchment paper.

4. Drop dough by rounded tablespoons (or use an ice cream scoop 1½ inches in diameter) 2 inches apart onto prepared baking sheets. Bake, one sheet at a time, 8 to 10 minutes or until browned around the edges. Cool on baking sheets 5 minutes. Transfer cookies to wire cooling racks to cool completely.

5. Using a spoon or offset spatula, spread a heaping teaspoon of peanut butter filling onto the flat side of a cookie, then top with the flat side of another cookie. Repeat to fill the remaining cookies.

Peanut Butter Sandwich Cookies
Classic • Family Favorite

Use traditional, not all-natural, peanut butter for these giant cookie sandwiches and spray the measuring cup with nonstick cooking spray so the peanut butter releases easily into the dough.

PREP   30 minutes
CHILL   2 hours
BAKE   8 to 10 minutes per batch
MAKES   15 cookie sandwiches

INGREDIENTS

1⅓ cups all-purpose flour
½ teaspoon baking powder
½ teaspoon baking soda
½ teaspoon kosher salt

quick tip

Refrigerating cookie dough before baking keeps cookies from spreading and improves their taste and texture.

Oatmeal, Dark Chocolate & Cherry Cookies

Easy • Nut-Free

Swapping dried cherries for raisins in these chewy, gooey and crunchy treats brings a classic cookie to a new level. The intense flavor of tart Montmorency cherries pairs well with dark chocolate, but any variety will be delicious. If you can't find Montmorency cherries in your local grocery store, you can order them on Amazon.

PREP 20 minutes
BAKE 12 to 13 minutes per batch
MAKES 3 dozen cookies

INGREDIENTS

- 1½ cups all-purpose flour
- 1 teaspoon baking soda
- ½ teaspoon kosher salt
- 1 cup (2 sticks) unsalted butter, at room temperature
- ¾ cup granulated sugar
- ¾ cup firmly packed light brown sugar
- 1 large egg
- 1 teaspoon vanilla extract
- 2 cups old-fashioned rolled oats (not quick cooking)
- 1 (10-ounce) bag bittersweet chocolate chips (about 1½ cups)
- 1 cup dried cherries, preferably Montmorency or other tart cherries

INSTRUCTIONS

1. Preheat oven to 350°F. Line 3 baking sheets with parchment paper. Set aside.

2. In a medium bowl, whisk together flour, baking soda and salt.

3. In a large bowl, using an electric mixer, beat butter and both sugars together on medium-high speed until pale and fluffy, about 2 minutes. Scrape down the sides of the bowl with a rubber spatula. Add egg and vanilla and beat on medium speed until incorporated. Add flour mixture and beat on low speed just until combined. Using a rubber spatula, stir in oats, chocolate chips and cherries.

4. Drop dough by rounded tablespoons (or use an ice cream scoop 1½ inches in diameter) about 2 inches apart onto prepared baking sheets. Bake, one sheet at a time, 12 to 13 minutes or until set and golden brown. Cool on baking sheets 1 to 2 minutes. Transfer cookies to wire cooling racks to cool completely.

Double Oatmeal-Chocolate Chunk Cookies

Easy • Family Favorite • Nut-Free

Although it's nut-free, oat flour adds a slightly nutty flavor and rich texture to a classic oatmeal-chocolate combination.

PREP 15 minutes

BAKE 10 minutes per batch

MAKES 3 dozen cookies

INGREDIENTS

- ¾ cup oat flour
- ¾ cup all-purpose flour
- 1 teaspoon baking soda
- ½ teaspoon kosher salt
- 1 cup (2 sticks) unsalted butter, at room temperature
- ¾ cup granulated sugar
- ¾ cup firmly packed light brown sugar
- 1 large egg
- 1 teaspoon vanilla extract
- 2 cups old-fashioned rolled oats (not quick cooking)
- 8 ounces semisweet or bittersweet chocolate, chopped into chunks

quick tip

Can't find oat flour? Make your own by blending whole rolled oats (not steel cut or quick oats) in a food processor or high-speed blender until it forms a fine flour.

INSTRUCTIONS

1. Preheat oven to 350°F. Line 3 baking sheets with parchment paper. Set aside.

2. In a medium bowl, whisk together the flours, baking soda and salt.

3. In a large bowl, using an electric mixer, beat butter and both sugars together on medium-high speed until pale and fluffy, about 2 minutes. Scrape down the sides of the bowl with a rubber spatula. Add egg and vanilla and beat on medium-high speed until well combined. Scrape down the sides of the bowl. Add flour mixture and beat on low speed just until combined. Using a rubber spatula, stir in oats and chocolate.

4. Drop dough by rounded tablespoons (or use an ice cream scoop 1½ inches in diameter) 2 inches apart onto prepared baking sheets. Refrigerate dough between batches if it gets too soft to prevent cookies from spreading. Bake, one sheet at a time, 10 minutes or until lightly golden brown around the edges. Cool on baking sheets 1 to 2 minutes. Transfer cookies to wire cooling racks to cool completely.

Chocolate Crackles

Family Favorite • Nut-Free

You can melt chocolate in the microwave in 30-second intervals, stirring between each, for about 2 minutes total.

PREP 20 minutes
CHILL 30 minutes to 1 hour
BAKE 12 minutes per batch
MAKES 1½ dozen cookies

INGREDIENTS

- ⅔ **cup all-purpose flour**
- ⅓ **cup unsweetened cocoa powder**
- 1 **teaspoon baking powder**
- ½ **teaspoon kosher salt**
- 4 **tablespoons (½ stick) unsalted butter, at room temperature**
- ¾ **cup firmly packed light brown sugar**
- 1 **large egg**
- ½ **teaspoon vanilla extract**
- 4 **ounces semisweet or bittersweet chocolate, melted and cooled**
- 2 **tablespoons whole milk**
- ¼ **cup granulated sugar**
- ¼ **cup confectioners' sugar**

INSTRUCTIONS

1. In a medium bowl, whisk together flour, cocoa powder, baking powder and salt.

2. In a large bowl, using an electric mixer, beat butter and brown sugar together on medium-high speed until fluffy, about 2 minutes. Scrape down the sides of the bowl with a rubber spatula. Add egg and vanilla and beat on medium-high speed until well combined. Add melted chocolate and beat until combined. Add flour mixture and milk and beat on low speed just until combined. Flatten dough into a disk, cover tightly with plastic wrap, and refrigerate until it's firm, about 30 minutes to 1 hour.

3. Preheat oven to 350°F. Line 2 baking sheets with parchment paper.

4. Place granulated and confectioners' sugars each in separate small bowls. Scoop rounded tablespoons of dough (or use an ice cream scoop 1½ inches in diameter) into the palms of your hands and roll into balls. Roll each ball in granulated sugar, then in confectioners' sugar. Place balls about 2 inches apart on prepared baking sheets. Bake, one sheet at a time, 12 minutes or until surfaces crack. Cool on baking sheets 5 minutes. Transfer cookies to wire cooling racks to cool completely.

Triple Chocolate-Chunk Cookies

Easy • Family Favorite
Make Ahead • Nut-Free

Use any ratio of dark, milk and white chocolate in these chewy beauties. You can purchase precut chocolate chunks, if you like, to save time.

PREP	20 minutes
CHILL	30 minutes or up to 2 days
BAKE	10 minutes per batch
MAKES	3½ dozen cookies

INGREDIENTS

- 2¼ cups all-purpose flour
- 1 teaspoon baking soda
- 1 teaspoon kosher salt
- 1 cup (2 sticks) unsalted butter, at room temperature
- ⅔ cup granulated sugar
- ⅔ cup firmly packed light brown sugar
- 2 large eggs
- 1½ teaspoons vanilla extract
- 4 ounces semisweet or bittersweet chocolate, chopped into chunks
- 4 ounces milk chocolate, chopped into chunks
- 4 ounces white chocolate, chopped into chunks

INSTRUCTIONS

1. In a medium bowl, whisk together flour, baking soda and salt.

2. In a large bowl, using an electric mixer, beat butter and both sugars together on medium-high speed until pale and fluffy, about 2 minutes. Scrape down the sides of the bowl with a rubber spatula. Add eggs and vanilla and beat on medium-high speed until well combined. Scrape down the sides of the bowl. Add flour mixture and beat on low speed just until combined. Using a rubber spatula, stir in chocolate chunks. Flatten dough into a disk, cover tightly with plastic wrap, and refrigerate at least 30 minutes or up to 2 days.

3. Preheat oven to 350°F. Line 3 baking sheets with parchment paper.

4. Drop dough by rounded tablespoons (or use an ice cream scoop 1½ inches in diameter) 2 inches apart onto prepared baking sheets. Bake, one sheet at a time, 10 minutes or until set and edges are light golden brown. Cool on baking sheets 5 minutes. Transfer cookies to wire cooling racks to cool completely.

NOTE This dough is best refrigerated overnight, but you can wait up to 2 days to bake the cookies.

Dark Chocolate-Cranberry Cookies

Easy • Family Favorite
Make Ahead • Nut-Free

Keep the dough in the fridge between batches to prevent the cookies from spreading too much when baking.

PREP 20 minutes
CHILL 30 minutes or up to 2 days
BAKE 10 to 12 minutes per batch
MAKES 3 dozen cookies

INGREDIENTS

- 2¼ cups all-purpose flour
- 1 teaspoon baking soda
- 1 teaspoon kosher salt
- 1 cup (2 sticks) unsalted butter, at room temperature
- ¾ cup granulated sugar
- ¾ cup firmly packed light brown sugar
- 2 large eggs
- 1 teaspoon vanilla extract
- 1 cup bittersweet chocolate chips
- 1 cup dried cranberries

INSTRUCTIONS

1. In a medium bowl, whisk together flour, baking soda and salt.
2. In a large bowl, using an electric mixer, beat butter and both sugars together on medium-high speed until pale and fluffy, about 2 minutes. Scrape down the sides of the bowl with a rubber spatula. Add eggs and vanilla and beat on medium-high speed until well combined. Add flour mixture and beat on low speed just until combined. Using a rubber spatula, stir in chocolate chips and cranberries. Flatten dough into a disk, cover tightly with plastic wrap, and refrigerate at least 30 minutes or up to 2 days.
3. Preheat oven to 350°F. Line 3 baking sheets with parchment.
4. Drop dough by rounded tablespoons (or use an ice cream scoop 1½ inches in diameter) 2 inches apart onto prepared baking sheets. Bake, one sheet at a time, 10 to 12 minutes or until edges are light golden brown. Cool on baking sheets 5 minutes. Transfer cookies to wire cooling racks to cool completely.

SNICKERDOODLES

Snickerdoodles

Classic • Easy • Family Favorite
Nut-Free

Try Vietnamese cinnamon for extra flavor and organic cane sugar for a crunchier topping.

PREP 15 minutes
BAKE 10 to 12 minutes per batch
MAKES 3½ to 4 dozen cookies

INGREDIENTS

- 3 cups all-purpose flour
- 1½ teaspoons baking powder
- ½ teaspoon kosher salt
- 1 cup (2 sticks) unsalted butter, at room temperature
- 1¾ cups sugar, divided
- 2 large eggs
- 1½ teaspoons vanilla extract
- 1 teaspoon ground cinnamon

INSTRUCTIONS

1. Preheat oven to 350°F. Line 3 baking sheets with parchment.
2. In a medium bowl, whisk together flour, baking powder and salt.
3. In a large bowl, using an electric mixer, beat butter and 1½ cups sugar together on medium-high speed until pale and fluffy, about 2 minutes. Scrape down the sides of the bowl with a rubber spatula. Add eggs and vanilla and beat on medium-high speed until well combined. Add flour mixture and beat on low speed just until combined.
4. In a small bowl, whisk together the remaining ¼ cup sugar and cinnamon.
5. Scoop rounded tablespoons of dough (or use an ice cream scoop 1½ inches in diameter) into the palms of your hands and roll into balls. Roll in the cinnamon-sugar mixture. Place balls 2 inches apart on prepared baking sheets. Bake, one sheet at a time, 10 to 12 minutes or until edges are lightly browned but tops are barely colored. Cool on baking sheets 5 minutes. Transfer cookies to wire cooling racks to cool completely.

quick tip

If you don't have lemon extract, replace the milk in the icing with fresh lemon juice instead.

Iced Lemon Drops

Easy • Family Favorite • Nut-Free

Lemon icing is the traditional topping for these cakelike cookies, but choose any flavor variation of the 5-Minute Icing that you like (see page 123).

PREP 15 minutes
BAKE 8 to 10 minutes per batch
MAKES 4 dozen cookies

INGREDIENTS

- 5 cups all-purpose flour
- 5 teaspoons baking powder
- 1 teaspoon kosher salt
- 1 cup (2 sticks) unsalted butter, at room temperature
- 1¼ cups sugar
- 6 large eggs
- 1 tablespoon vanilla extract
  5-Minute Lemon Icing (page 123)
  Rainbow or Christmas-colored nonpareil sprinkles, for decorating

INSTRUCTIONS

1. Preheat oven to 350°F. Line 3 baking sheets with parchment paper and set aside.

2. In a large bowl, whisk together flour, baking powder and salt.

3. In another large bowl, using an electric mixer, beat butter and sugar together on medium-high speed until pale and fluffy, about 2 minutes. Scrape down the sides of the bowl with a rubber spatula. Add eggs, one at a time, and beat on medium-high speed after each addition until well combined. Add vanilla and beat until incorporated. Scrape down the sides of the bowl. Gradually add flour mixture and beat on low speed just until combined.

4. Scoop rounded tablespoons of dough (or use an ice cream scoop 1½ inches in diameter) and roll into balls. Place balls 2 inches apart onto prepared baking sheets. Bake, one sheet at a time, 8 to 10 minutes or until set and puffed. (It's OK if they crack a little while baking.) Cool on baking sheets 1 to 2 minutes. Transfer cookies to wire cooling racks to cool completely.

5. Using a small spoon, spread icing on top of each cookie. While icing is still wet, sprinkle with nonpareils.

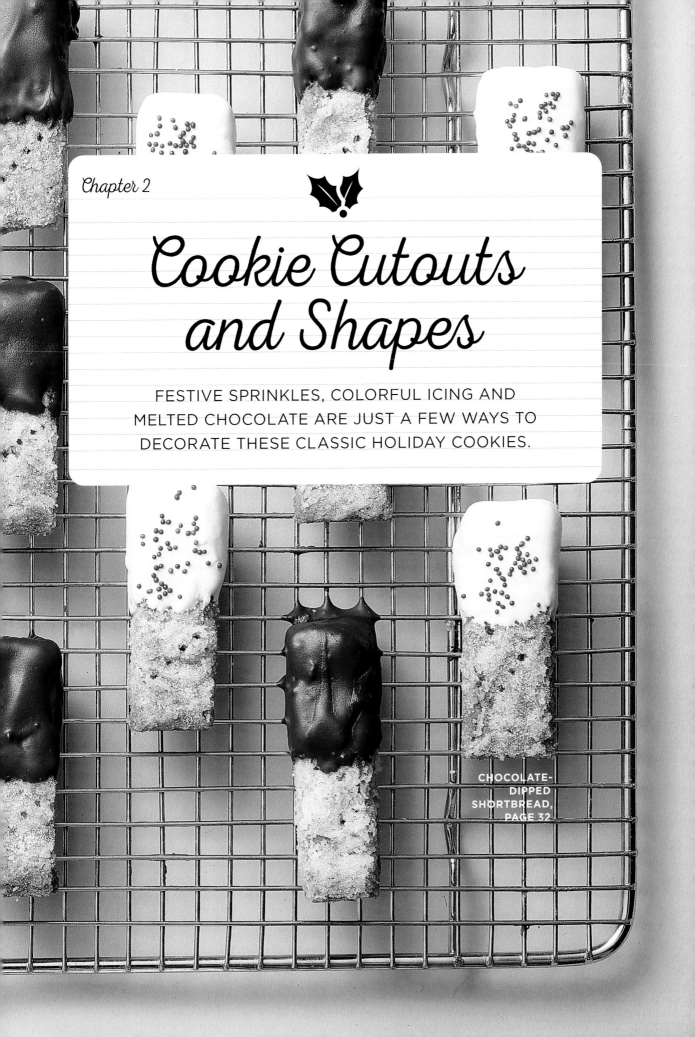

Chapter 2

Cookie Cutouts and Shapes

FESTIVE SPRINKLES, COLORFUL ICING AND MELTED CHOCOLATE ARE JUST A FEW WAYS TO DECORATE THESE CLASSIC HOLIDAY COOKIES.

CHOCOLATE-DIPPED SHORTBREAD, PAGE 32

Sprinkle Sugar Cookies

Family Favorite • Make Ahead
Nut-Free

Rolling sugar cookie dough in sprinkles before baking creates a colorful, kid-friendly treat.

PREP 20 minutes
CHILL 1 hour or up to overnight
BAKE 12 to 16 minutes per batch
MAKES 3 dozen cookies

INGREDIENTS

- 3 cups all-purpose flour, plus more for dusting
- 1 teaspoon baking powder
- ½ teaspoon kosher salt
- 1 cup (2 sticks) unsalted butter, at room temperature
- 1¼ cups sugar
- 1 large egg
- 2 teaspoons vanilla extract
- ¼ cup whole milk
- 1 cup colored sanding sugar or sprinkles

INSTRUCTIONS

1. In a medium bowl, whisk together flour, baking powder and salt.

2. In a large bowl, using an electric mixer, beat butter and sugar together on medium-high speed until light and fluffy, about 2 minutes. Add egg and vanilla and beat until combined. Scrape down the sides of the bowl with a rubber spatula. Add flour mixture, 1 cup at a time, and milk and beat on low speed just until combined. Flatten dough into a disk, cover tightly with plastic wrap, and refrigerate until firm, at least 1 hour or up to overnight.

3. Preheat oven to 350°F. Line 3 baking sheets with parchment paper.

4. Let dough sit at room temperature for 5 minutes to soften slightly. Place sugar or sprinkles in a small bowl. Scoop rounded tablespoons of dough (or use an ice cream scoop 1½ inches in diameter) into the palm of your hands and roll into balls. Roll each ball in sugar. Place balls 2 inches apart on prepared baking sheets. Use your fingers to slightly flatten balls into disks.

5. Bake, 1 sheet at a time, 12 to 16 minutes or until cookies are set and edges are light golden brown. Cool on baking sheets 5 minutes. Transfer cookies to wire cooling racks to cool completely.

NOTE You can use cookie cutters to cut shapes from the flattened disks before baking. Stick with simple shapes, such as hearts, then sprinkle with sugar.

White Chocolate, Cranberry & Nut Biscotti

**Company–Worthy • Family Favorite
Gift Idea • Make Ahead**

These crispy, dunkable cookies get their name from being baked twice. The final result will last for two weeks in an airtight container, making them perfect for gifting.

PREP 10 minutes

BAKE 42 to 50 minutes, per batch, in two parts

MAKES 3 dozen cookies

INGREDIENTS

- 2¾ cups all-purpose flour, plus more for dusting
- 2 teaspoons baking powder
- 1 teaspoon ground cinnamon
- ½ teaspoon ground ginger
- ½ teaspoon ground nutmeg
  Pinch of ground cloves
- 1¼ cups sugar
- ½ teaspoon kosher salt
- 3 eggs, lightly beaten
- ½ cup (1 stick) unsalted butter, melted and cooled to room temperature
- 1 teaspoon vanilla extract
  Freshly grated zest of 1 orange
- 4 ounces white chocolate, cut into chunks
- 1 cup coarsely chopped pistachios, almonds or hazelnuts, or a combination
- ½ cup dried cranberries

quick tip
If you have an extra-large baking sheet, you can bake all three logs at the same time for the first bake.

INSTRUCTIONS

1. Preheat oven to 350°F. Line 2 baking sheets with parchment paper.

2. In large bowl, whisk together flour, baking powder, cinnamon, ginger, nutmeg, cloves, sugar and salt.

3. Using a rubber spatula, mix in eggs, butter, vanilla and orange zest until dough comes together. Fold in chocolate, nuts and cranberries and knead with your hands until evenly distributed and no flour remains.

4. Divide the dough evenly into three pieces. On a lightly floured work surface, shape each into a 10-inch-long log. Place logs 3 inches apart on prepared baking sheets, then gently flatten to 3 inches wide.

5. Bake, 1 sheet at a time, 20 to 25 minutes or until crisp and light golden brown on the outside but still soft in the center. Cool on baking sheets 10 minutes. Reduce oven temperature to 300°F.

6. Transfer the logs to a cutting board. Using a serrated knife, cut on the diagonal into slices about ¾ inch thick. Place slices, cut-side down, ½ inch apart on prepared baking sheets. Bake, one sheet at a time, until golden, about 12 minutes, then flip and bake 10 to 12 minutes longer. Cool on baking sheets 5 minutes, then transfer to wire cooling racks to cool completely. Centers will firm while cooling.

quick tip

Metal cookie cutters will create the cleanest edges when cutting dough. Dip them in flour if the dough starts to stick.

Chocolate-Dipped Shortbread

Classic • Gift Idea • Nut-Free

Dipping these buttery cookies into melted dark or white chocolate (or both!) will make these the envy of every cookie swap.

PREP 10 minutes
BAKE 1 hour
MAKES 27 cookies

INGREDIENTS

- 1½ cups all-purpose flour
- ¼ teaspoon kosher salt
- 1 cup (2 sticks) unsalted butter, at room temperature
- ½ cup sugar, plus more for sprinkling
- 2 teaspoons vanilla extract
- 6 ounces semisweet or white chocolate, or a combination, melted
  Colored sprinkles, for decorating (optional)

INSTRUCTIONS

1. Preheat oven to 325°F. Lightly coat a 9-inch-square baking pan with butter or nonstick cooking spray.
2. In a medium bowl, whisk together flour and salt.
3. In a large bowl, using an electric mixer, beat butter on high speed until fluffy, about 2 minutes. Add sugar and beat until combined. Beat in vanilla. Scrape down the sides of the bowl with a rubber spatula. Add flour mixture and beat on low speed just until combined.
4. Using floured fingers, press dough into even layer in prepared pan. Sprinkle evenly with sugar.
5. Bake until edges are golden, about 1 hour. Using a sharp knife, immediately cut shortbread into 3- x 1-inch bars, and poke evenly with tines of a fork while still in pan. Cool in pan 30 minutes, then transfer cookies to wire rack to cool completely.
6. Set a wire rack atop a baking sheet lined with parchment paper (this will make for easy cleanup). Place melted chocolate in a small, deep bowl. Dunk half of each cookie into the chocolate, twisting the cookie after each dunk so the chocolate doesn't drip, and place on wire rack to set. Decorate with sprinkles (if using) while chocolate is still wet.

Classic Sugar Cookies

**Family Favorite • Make Ahead
Nut-Free**

The holiday season wouldn't be complete without dozens of decorated sugar cookies. Start by perfecting the classic dough (below), then try your hand at different decorating techniques (page 35).

PREP 15 minutes
CHILL 1 hour or up to overnight
BAKE 12 to 16 minutes per batch
MAKES about 3 dozen cookies

INGREDIENTS

- 3 cups all-purpose flour, plus more for dusting
- 1 teaspoon baking powder
- ½ teaspoon kosher salt
- 1 cup (2 sticks) unsalted butter, at room temperature
- 1¼ cups sugar
- 1 large egg
- 2 teaspoons vanilla extract
- 2 tablespoons whole milk

INSTRUCTIONS

1. In a medium bowl, whisk together flour, baking powder and salt.
2. In a large bowl, using an electric mixer, beat butter and sugar together on medium-high speed until light and fluffy, about 2 minutes. Add egg and vanilla and beat until combined. Scrape down the sides of the bowl with a rubber spatula. Add flour mixture, 1 cup at a time, and milk and beat on low speed just until combined. Flatten dough into a disk, cover tightly with plastic wrap, and refrigerate until firm, at least 1 hour or up to overnight.
3. Preheat oven to 350°F. Line 3 baking sheets with parchment paper.
4. Lightly dust a clean work surface with flour. Let dough sit at room temperature for 5 minutes. Dust a rolling pin with flour and roll dough into a ¼-inch-thick rectangle. Use cookie cutters to cut out shapes. Place cutouts 1 inch apart on prepared baking sheets. Re-roll dough scraps to cut out additional shapes.
5. Bake, 1 sheet at a time, 12 to 16 minutes or until edges are set and light golden brown. Cool on baking sheets 5 minutes. Transfer cookies to wire racks to cool completely.
6. Once cool, decorate the cookies, as desired.
NOTE You can freeze dough, covered tightly in plastic wrap and stored in a freezer-safe zip-close bag, for up to 1 month. Let the dough thaw in the refrigerator before baking.

ICED
SUGAR
COOKIES

Iced Sugar Cookies
Family Favorite • Make Ahead Nut-Free

Once you bake and cool Classic Sugar Cookies (page 32), the fun begins! Decorate cutouts with white or colored royal icing and top with sprinkles, sanding sugar (which has coarse grains so it adds sparkle) and any other decorations you'd like. Here are some simple-to-master techniques to give your cookies a bakeshop look.

MAKES about 3 dozen cookies

INGREDIENTS

    Classic Sugar Cookies (page 32), baked and cooled
    Royal Icing (page 122)
    Gel food coloring (optional)
    Sprinkles and/or sanding sugar, for decorating (optional)

INSTRUCTIONS

1. Line baking sheets with parchment paper. Place cookies on sheets (this will make cleanup easier).
2. If making colored icing, divide royal icing among small bowls, one bowl for each color. Add food coloring, a few drops at a time, and stir with a spoon or rubber spatula until desired color is achieved. Cover bowls with plastic wrap until ready to use.
3. Fit pastry bag with desired piping tip. Fill bag with icing, a maximum of two-thirds full, leaving enough room on top to twist the bag closed.
4. To "flood" cookies, first pipe icing around the cookie's edge to form a border. Then pipe icing into the center of the cookie and let it run toward the border. Gently tap cookie on work surface so icing settles in a smooth, even layer. Decorate with sprinkles and/or sanding sugar, if using, as desired.

Icing will harden completely after about 6 hours.
5. If decorating with another color(s) on top of the first color (for example, the features on gingerbread people, decorations on Christmas trees, etc.), let first layer of icing set at room temperature until partially hardened, about 2 hours.
6. If you want to create a swirl pattern (like the snowflakes at left), while first layer of icing is still wet, pipe horizontal parallel lines across cookie with different color(s) of icing. Lightly drag tip of a toothpick from top to bottom through horizontal lines, creating evenly spaced vertical lines. Wipe toothpick clean, then drag it from bottom to top between the vertical lines. Wipe toothpick clean, as needed, to prevent smudging.
NOTE To save time, you can decorate sugar cookies with any flavor of 5-Minute Icing (page 123). Be sure the icing is thick enough so it doesn't run off the cookies.

Spiced Butter Cookies
Gift Idea • Make Ahead • Nut-Free

A dash of holiday spices and a coating of sesame seeds transforms classic butter cookies.

PREP 20 minutes
CHILL 1 to 1½ hours
BAKE 14 to 18 minutes per batch
MAKES 4 dozen cookies

INGREDIENTS

  2 cups all-purpose flour, plus more for dusting
  ½ teaspoon ground allspice
  ¼ teaspoon ground ginger
  ½ teaspoon kosher salt
  1 cup (2 sticks) unsalted butter, at room temperature
  1 cup confectioners' sugar
  1 teaspoon vanilla extract
    Sesame seeds, for rolling (optional)

quick tip
Gel food coloring is more concentrated than liquid, and will give frostings and icings richer hues.

INSTRUCTIONS

1. In a medium bowl, whisk together flour, allspice, ginger and salt.
2. In a large bowl, using an electric mixer, beat butter, sugar and vanilla together on medium-high speed until light and fluffy, about 2 minutes. Scrape down sides of the bowl with a rubber spatula. Add flour mixture and beat on low speed just until combined.
3. Lightly flour a clean work surface. Divide dough in half. Roll each half into a log about 1½ inches in diameter, then roll logs in sesame seeds, if using, to coat. Wrap logs tightly in parchment or wax paper, and refrigerate until firm, 1 to 1½ hours.
4. Preheat oven to 350°F. Line 2 baking sheets with parchment paper.
5. Let dough rest at room temperature for 10 minutes. Using a serrated knife, slice each log into ⅜-inch-thick rounds. Place slices 1 inch apart on prepared baking sheets.
6. Bake, 1 sheet at a time, 14 to 18 minutes or until edges are light golden brown. Cool on baking sheets 5 minutes. Transfer cookies to wire cooling racks to cool completely.

Vanilla Shortbread

Gift Idea • Nut-Free

These classic cookies are a holiday favorite, but they're delicious any time. Gift them with an assortment of herbal teas.

PREP   10 minutes
BAKE   1 hour
MAKES   27 cookies

INGREDIENTS

- 1½ cups all-purpose flour
- ¼ teaspoon kosher salt
- 1 cup (2 sticks) unsalted butter, at room temperature
- ½ cup sugar, plus more for sprinkling
- 2 teaspoons vanilla extract

INSTRUCTIONS

1. Preheat oven to 325°F. Lightly coat a 9-inch-square baking pan with butter or nonstick cooking spray.

2. In a medium bowl, whisk together flour and salt.

3. In a large bowl, using an electric mixer, beat butter on high speed until fluffy, about 2 minutes. Add sugar and beat until combined. Beat in vanilla. Scrape down the sides of the bowl with a rubber spatula. Add flour mixture and beat on low speed just until combined.

4. Using floured fingers, press dough into even layer in prepared pan. Sprinkle evenly with sugar.

5. Bake until edges are golden, about 1 hour. Using a sharp knife, immediately cut shortbread into 3- x 1-inch bars, and poke evenly with tines of a fork while still in pan. Cool in pan 30 minutes, then transfer cookies to wire rack to cool completely.

Chocolate-Dipped Butter Cookies With Crushed Candy Canes

Family Favorite • Nut-Free

You can sub chocolate chips for the chocolate bar.

PREP 20 minutes
CHILL 1 to 1½ hours
BAKE 14 to 18 minutes per batch
MAKES 4 dozen cookies

INGREDIENTS

- 1 cup (2 sticks) unsalted butter, at room temperature
- 1 cup confectioners' sugar
- 1 teaspoon vanilla extract
- ½ teaspoon kosher salt
- 2 cups all-purpose flour, plus more for dusting
- 8 ounces semisweet chocolate, melted
- Crushed candy canes or peppermint candies

INSTRUCTIONS

1. In a large bowl, using an electric mixer, beat butter, sugar, vanilla and salt together on medium-high speed until light and fluffy, about 2 minutes. Scrape down sides of the bowl with a rubber spatula. Add flour and beat on low speed just until combined.

2. Lightly flour a clean work surface. Divide dough in half. Roll each half into a log about 1½ inches in diameter. Wrap each log tightly in parchment or wax paper, and refrigerate until firm, 1 to 1½ hours.

3. Preheat oven to 350°F. Line 2 baking sheets with parchment paper.

4. Let dough rest at room temperature for 10 minutes. Using a serrated knife, slice each log into ⅜-inch-thick rounds. Place slices 1 inch apart on baking sheets.

5. Bake, 1 sheet at a time, 14 to 18 minutes or until edges are light golden brown. Cool on baking sheets 5 minutes. Transfer to wire cooling racks to cool completely.

6. Set a wire rack atop a baking sheet lined with parchment paper (this will make for easy cleanup). Place melted chocolate in a small, deep bowl. Dunk half of each cookie into the chocolate, twisting the cookie after each dunk so the chocolate doesn't drip, and place on wire rack to set. Decorate with crushed candy canes while chocolate is still wet.

Cookie Cutouts and Shapes

ICED GINGERSNAPS

Iced Gingersnaps

Classic • Family Favorite
Make Ahead • Nut-Free

You can keep this forgiving dough in the refrigerator for up to 2 days before baking. Unlike other doughs made with butter, it holds its shape for a while at room temperature, making it ideal for little hands to use.

PREP 20 minutes
CHILL 2 hours or up to 2 days
BAKE 8 to 10 minutes per batch
MAKES about 4 dozen cookies

INGREDIENTS

- ¾ cup dark corn syrup
- ¾ cup water
- 1 tablespoon cinnamon
- 1 tablespoon ground cloves
- 1 tablespoon ground ginger
- 6 cups all-purpose flour, plus more for dusting
- 1 tablespoon baking soda
- ¼ teaspoon kosher salt
- 1 cup (2 sticks) unsalted butter, at room temperature
- 2½ cups sugar
  5-Minute Icing (page 123), for decorating (optional)
  Sprinkles and/or sanding sugar, for decorating (optional)

INSTRUCTIONS

1. In a medium saucepan set on the stovetop over medium heat, combine corn syrup, water, cinnamon, cloves and ginger. Bring to a boil, stirring occasionally until spices are dissolved. Remove from heat and let cool slightly.

2. In a large bowl, whisk together flour, baking soda and salt.

3. In another large bowl, using an electric mixer, beat butter and sugar together on medium-high speed until light and fluffy, about 2 minutes. Add spice mixture and beat on medium speed until combined. Scrape down the sides of the bowl with a rubber spatula. Add flour mixture and beat on low speed just until combined. Do not overmix. Divide dough in half, shape each half into a disk, cover tightly with plastic wrap and refrigerate until firm, at least 2 hours or up to 2 days.

4. Preheat oven to 350°F. Line 2 baking sheets with parchment paper.

5. Lightly dust a clean work surface with flour. Working with one disk at a time, dust rolling pin with flour and roll dough into a ¼-inch-thick rectangle. Use cookie cutters to cut out shapes. Place cutouts 1 inch apart on prepared baking sheets. Re-roll dough scraps to cut out additional shapes.

6. Bake, 1 sheet at a time, 8 to 10 minutes or until cookies darken in color and edges are crisp. Cool on baking sheets 5 minutes. Transfer cookies to wire racks to cool completely.

7. While cookies cool, make the icing. Use a spoon to spread icing evenly on top of cookies. While icing is still wet, decorate with sprinkles or sanding sugar, if using.

Chocolate Sugar Cookies

Family Favorite • Make Ahead
Nut-Free

These sweet treats are delectable as is, or decorate them with icing and sprinkles as you would traditional sugar cookies.

PREP 15 minutes
CHILL 1 hour or up to overnight
BAKE 12 to 16 minutes per batch
MAKES about 3 dozen cookies

INGREDIENTS

- 2¼ cups all-purpose flour
- ⅓ cup unsweetened cocoa powder
- ½ teaspoon baking powder
- ½ teaspoon baking soda
- ½ teaspoon kosher salt
- ¾ cup (1½ sticks) unsalted butter, at room temperature
- ¾ cup firmly packed light brown sugar
- ½ cup granulated sugar
- 1 large egg
- 2 teaspoons vanilla extract
  Royal Icing (page 122)
  Gel food coloring (optional)

INSTRUCTIONS

1. In a medium bowl, whisk together flour, cocoa powder, baking powder, baking soda and salt.

2. In a large bowl, using an electric mixer, beat butter and both sugars together on medium-high speed until light and fluffy, about 2 minutes. Add egg and vanilla and beat until combined. Scrape down the sides of the bowl with a rubber spatula. Add flour mixture and beat on low speed just until combined. Flatten dough into a disk, cover tightly with plastic wrap, and refrigerate until firm, at least 1 hour or up to overnight.

3. Preheat oven to 350°F. Line 3 baking sheets with parchment paper.

4. Lightly dust a clean work surface with flour. Let dough sit at room temperature for 5 minutes. Dust a rolling pin with flour (don't use too much or dough will change color) and roll dough into a ¼-inch-thick rectangle. Use cookie cutters to cut out shapes. Place cutouts 1 inch apart on prepared baking sheets. Re-roll dough scraps to cut out additional shapes.

5. Bake, 1 sheet at a time, 12 to 16 minutes or until firm. Cool on baking sheets 5 minutes. Transfer cookies to wire racks to cool completely.

6. For decorating ideas using colored royal icing, see page 35.

Stained Glass Stars

Classic • Family Favorite
Nut-Free

You'll need two sizes of cookie cutters to create these showstopping treats. These stars are festive, but any shapes will work. (Bake the cutouts, too!)

PREP 15 minutes
CHILL 1 hour or up to overnight
BAKE 14 to 16 minutes per batch
MAKES 3 dozen cookies

INGREDIENTS

- 3 cups all-purpose flour, plus more for dusting
- 1 teaspoon baking powder
- ½ teaspoon kosher salt
- 1 cup (2 sticks) unsalted butter, at room temperature
- 1¼ cups sugar
- 1 large egg
- 2 teaspoons vanilla extract
- 2 tablespoons whole milk
- 1 (7-ounce) bag assorted colored hard candies, such as Jolly Ranchers

INSTRUCTIONS

1. In a medium bowl, whisk together flour, baking powder and salt.

2. In a large bowl, using an electric mixer, beat butter and sugar together on medium-high speed until light and fluffy, about 2 minutes. Add egg and vanilla and beat until combined. Scrape down the sides of the bowl with a rubber spatula. Add flour mixture, 1 cup at a time, alternating with milk, and beat on low speed just until combined. Flatten dough into a disk, cover tightly with plastic wrap, and refrigerate until firm, at least 1 hour or up to overnight.

3. Preheat oven to 350°F. Line 3 baking sheets with parchment paper.

4. Separate hard candies by color and place each in a sealed zip-close plastic bag. Use a rolling pin to gently crush the candies. Set aside.

5. Lightly dust a clean work surface with flour. Let dough sit at room temperature for 5 minutes. Dust a rolling pin with flour and roll dough into a ¼-inch-thick rectangle. Use larger cookie cutters to cut out shapes. Use smaller cookie cutters to cut out a window from each shape and remove the dough from that area. Place cookies and cutouts 1 inch apart on prepared baking sheets. Re-roll dough scraps to cut out additional shapes.

6. Bake, 1 sheet at a time, 8 minutes. Remove baking sheet from oven and spoon crushed candies into cutout centers. Return to oven and bake 6 to 8 minutes longer, or until candy is set and edges are light golden brown. Cool completely on baking sheets.

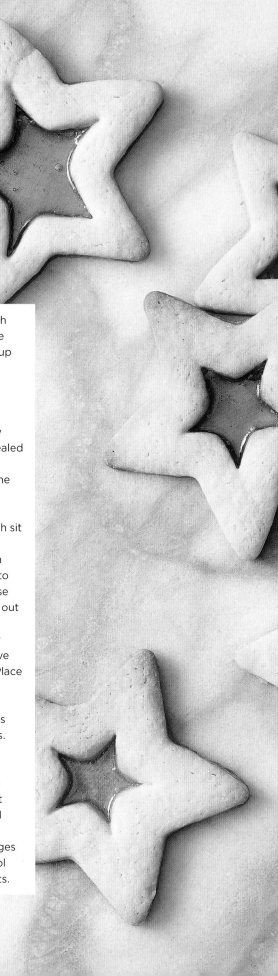

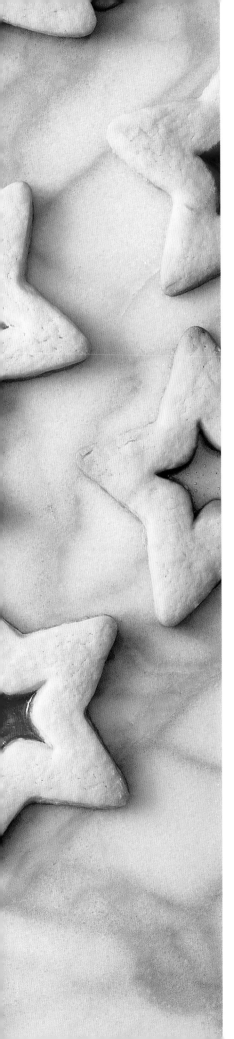

Slice-and-Bake Butter Cookies

Family Favorite • Make Ahead Nut-Free

You can freeze these dough logs, unbaked and wrapped well, for up to six months.

PREP 20 minutes
CHILL 1 to 1½ hours
BAKE 14 to 18 minutes per batch
MAKES 4 dozen cookies

INGREDIENTS

- 1 cup (2 sticks) unsalted butter, at room temperature
- 1 cup confectioners' sugar
- 1 teaspoon vanilla extract
- ½ teaspoon kosher salt
- 2 cups all-purpose flour, plus more for dusting
  Sanding sugar, for rolling

INSTRUCTIONS

1. In a large bowl, using an electric mixer, beat butter, sugar, vanilla and salt together on medium-high speed until light and fluffy, about 2 minutes. Scrape down sides of the bowl with a rubber spatula. Add flour and beat on low speed just until combined.

2. Lightly flour a clean work surface. Divide dough in half. Roll each half into a log about 1½ inches in diameter, then roll each log in sanding sugar to coat. Wrap each log tightly in parchment or wax paper, and refrigerate until firm, 1 to 1½ hours.

3. Preheat oven to 350°F. Line 2 baking sheets with parchment paper.

4. Let dough rest at room temperature for 10 minutes. Using a serrated knife, slice each log into ⅜-inch-thick rounds. Place slices 1 inch apart on prepared baking sheets.

5. Bake, 1 sheet at a time, 14 to 18 minutes or until edges are light golden brown. Cool on baking sheets 5 minutes. Transfer cookies to wire cooling racks to cool completely.

41

Linzer Cookies
Classic • Family Favorite

Use any flavor of jam inside these nutty, buttery treats; you can swap the almonds for hazelnuts, if you like.

PREP 15 minutes
CHILL 1 hour or up to overnight
BAKE 14 to 15 minutes per batch
MAKES 1 dozen sandwich cookies

INGREDIENTS

- 1 cup blanched almonds
- 2 cups all-purpose flour, plus more for dusting
- 1 teaspoon baking powder
- 1 teaspoon ground cinnamon
- Pinch of ground nutmeg
- ½ teaspoon kosher salt
- 1 cup (2 sticks) unsalted butter, at room temperature
- ⅔ cup granulated sugar
- 2 large egg yolks
- ½ teaspoon vanilla extract
- Raspberry, strawberry, blackberry or apricot jam, for filling
- Confectioners' sugar, for dusting

INSTRUCTIONS

1. In a food processor, pulse almonds until finely ground.
2. In a medium bowl, whisk together ground almonds, flour, baking powder, cinnamon, nutmeg and salt.
3. In a large bowl, using an electric mixer, beat butter and granulated sugar together on medium-high speed until light and fluffy, about 2 minutes. Add egg yolks and vanilla and beat until combined. Scrape down sides of the bowl with a rubber spatula. Add flour mixture and beat on low speed just until combined. Divide dough in half, flatten each into a disk, cover tightly with plastic wrap, and refrigerate until firm, at least 1 hour or up to overnight.

4. Preheat oven to 325°F. Line 2 baking sheets with parchment paper.
5. Let dough rest at room temperature for 5 to 10 minutes to soften. Lightly dust dough with flour. Working with 1 piece at a time, roll dough between 2 sheets of wax or parchment paper into a ⅛-inch-thick rectangle. Remove top layer of paper and use cookie cutters to cut out shapes. Using smaller cookie cutters, cut out a center from half of the shapes and remove the dough from that area. (If dough becomes too sticky, transfer to a prepared baking sheet and freeze for 10 minutes, either before or after cutting shapes.) Place cookies and cutouts 1 inch apart on prepared baking sheets. Re-roll dough scraps to cut out additional shapes.
6. Bake, 1 sheet at a time, 14 to 15 minutes or until crisp and lightly golden all over. Transfer cookies to wire cooling racks to cool completely.
7. Spread jam evenly over flat sides of whole cookies. Top each with a cutout cookie and sprinkle with confectioners' sugar.

quick tip
Ground nuts make this dough quite fragile. If it becomes too sticky or hard to work with when rolling or cutting out shapes, freeze it for about 10 minutes.

CHOCOLATE SANDWICH
COOKIES

Chocolate Sandwich Cookies

Family Favorite • Make Ahead
Nut-Free

Fill these crispy chocolate rounds with chocolate, white chocolate or cream filling—or a combination of them all!

PREP 10 minutes
CHILL 1 hour or up to overnight
BAKE 10 to 12 minutes per batch
MAKES 2 dozen sandwich cookies

INGREDIENTS

- 1 cup unsweetened cocoa powder
- ⅔ cup all-purpose flour, plus more for dusting
- ½ teaspoon kosher salt
- ½ cup (1 stick) unsalted butter, at room temperature
- ½ cup sugar
- 1 large egg
- ½ teaspoon vanilla extract Chocolate Ganache (page 125), Cream Filling (page 124) or White Chocolate Filling (page 124)

INSTRUCTIONS

1. In a medium bowl, whisk together cocoa powder, flour and salt.
2. In a large bowl, using an electric mixer, beat butter and sugar together on medium-high speed until light and fluffy, about 2 minutes. Add egg and vanilla and beat until combined. Scrape down sides of the bowl with a rubber spatula. Add flour mixture and beat on low speed just until combined. Divide dough in half, flatten each into a disk, cover tightly with plastic wrap, and refrigerate until firm, at least 1 hour or up to overnight.
3. Preheat oven to 350°F. Line 2 baking sheets with parchment paper.
4. Lightly dust a clean work surface with flour. (Don't use too much or dough will change color.) Working with 1 piece at a time, roll dough into a ⅛-inch-thick rectangle. Use a 2-inch round cookie cutter to cut out circles from the dough. Place rounds 1 inch apart on prepared baking sheets. Re-roll dough scraps to cut out additional circles.
5. Bake, 1 sheet at a time, 10 to 12 minutes or until firm. Cool completely on baking sheets on wire racks.
6. When cool, make the filling(s). Spoon about 1 teaspoon of filling onto bottom of one cookie and top with another cookie.

Pecan Butter Cookies

Easy • Family Favorite
Make Ahead

Toast pecans on a rimmed baking sheet in the oven for 7 to 10 minutes at 350°F, tossing occasionally. Toasting brings out their flavor.

PREP 20 minutes
CHILL 1 to 1½ hours
BAKE 14 to 18 minutes per batch
MAKES 4 dozen cookies

INGREDIENTS

- 2 cups all-purpose flour, plus more for dusting
- ½ cup toasted pecans, finely chopped
- ½ teaspoon kosher salt
- 1 cup (2 sticks) unsalted butter, at room temperature
- 1 cup confectioners' sugar
- 1 teaspoon vanilla extract

INSTRUCTIONS

1. In a medium bowl, whisk together flour, pecans and salt.
2. In a large bowl, using an electric mixer, beat butter, sugar and vanilla together on medium-high speed until light and fluffy, about 2 minutes. Scrape down sides of the bowl with a rubber spatula. Add flour mixture and beat on low speed just until combined.
3. Lightly flour a clean work surface. Divide dough in half. Roll each half into a log about 1½ inches in diameter. Wrap each log tightly in parchment or wax paper, and refrigerate until firm, 1 to 1½ hours.
4. Preheat oven to 350°F. Line 2 baking sheets with parchment paper.
5. Let dough rest at room temperature for 10 minutes. Using a serrated knife, slice each log into ⅜-inch-thick rounds. Place the slices 1 inch apart on prepared baking sheets.
6. Bake, 1 sheet at a time, 14 to 18 minutes or until edges are light golden brown. Cool on baking sheets 5 minutes. Transfer cookies to wire cooling racks to cool completely.

quick tip
When filling the sandwiches, leave a little room around the edge of the bottom cookie so the filling doesn't ooze out.

Panettone Cookies
Classic • Make Ahead

Store these fruitcake-inspired treats in an airtight container for up to one week.

PREP 15 minutes
BAKE 60 to 70 minutes, in two parts
CHILL 30 to 45 minutes
MAKES 5 dozen cookies

INGREDIENTS
3 cups all-purpose flour
1 teaspoon baking powder
½ teaspoon kosher salt
1 large egg, plus
 1 large egg yolk
1 cup sugar
½ cup (1 stick) unsalted butter, melted and cooled to room temperature
1 teaspoon anise or vanilla extract
1 cup whole milk
½ cup pine nuts, lightly toasted
½ cup golden raisins
 Freshly grated zest of 1 lemon
1 teaspoon anise seeds

INSTRUCTIONS
1. Preheat oven to 350°F. Line four 3- x 5½-inch loaf pans with parchment paper.
2. In a medium bowl, whisk together flour, baking powder and salt.
3. In a large bowl, using an electric mixer, beat egg, yolk and sugar on medium speed until thick and pale yellow, about 2 minutes. Add melted butter and anise extract and beat until combined. Using a rubber spatula, stir in half the flour mixture. Stir in half the milk, then the remaining flour, and then the remaining milk. Gently fold in the pine nuts, raisins, lemon zest and anise seeds. Divide the batter evenly between prepared pans. Smooth top with a rubber or offset spatula.
4. Bake until golden brown and toothpick inserted into center comes out clean, 30 to 35 minutes. Cool in pans on wire rack 10 minutes, then remove from pans and place on rack to cool completely. When cool, put loaves in the freezer to firm up, 30 to 45 minutes.
5. Preheat oven to 300°F. Line 3 baking sheets with parchment. Remove loaves from freezer and cut each crosswise into ¼-inch-thick slices. Place slices ½ inch apart on baking sheets.
6. Bake, 1 sheet at a time, 30 to 35 minutes or until edges are crisp and light golden brown, flipping slices over halfway through baking. Cool on baking sheets 5 minutes. Transfer cookies to wire cooling racks to cool completely.

quick tip
You can toast pine nuts in a dry skillet on the stovetop over low heat until light golden brown, stirring occasionally, 5 to 8 minutes.

SUGAR COOKIE
BARS, PAGE 53

Chapter 3

Bar Cookies

THICK AND GOOEY, FUDGY AND CHEWY,
THESE PACKABLE BARS AND SQUARES
ARE PERFECT FOR GIFTING.

Chocolate Chip Blondies

Easy • Family Favorite • Nut-Free

This bar version of a chocolate chip cookie comes together in minutes. You could swap the semisweet for white chocolate chips, if you like.

PREP 10 minutes
BAKE 25 to 30 minutes
MAKES 16 bars

INGREDIENTS

- 1½ cups all-purpose flour
- 1 teaspoon baking powder
- ½ teaspoon kosher salt
- 1 cup (2 sticks) unsalted butter, at room temperature
- 1 cup firmly packed light brown sugar
- 2 large eggs
- 1 teaspoon vanilla extract
- 1 cup semisweet chocolate chips

INSTRUCTIONS

1. Preheat oven to 350°F. Coat an 8-inch-square baking pan with nonstick cooking spray or butter.
2. In a medium bowl, whisk together flour, baking powder and salt.
3. In a large bowl, using an electric mixer, beat butter and sugar together on medium-high speed until pale and fluffy, about 2 minutes. Add eggs and vanilla and beat until well combined. Add flour mixture and beat on low speed just until combined. Using a rubber spatula, stir in chocolate chips. Pour batter into prepared pan.
4. Bake blondies until a toothpick inserted into center comes out clean, 25 to 30 minutes. Cool completely on wire rack, then cut into bars.

Pecan Bars

Family Favorite • Gift Idea
Make Ahead

A gooey, sweet topping fills an easy, parbaked crust, resulting in scrumptious bars that can be wrapped individually for a cookie swap or given as gifts.

PREP 25 minutes

CHILL 15 minutes

BAKE 35 to 45 minutes, in two parts

MAKES 16 bars

INGREDIENTS

For the crust

- 1½ cups all-purpose flour
- ¼ cup granulated sugar
- ½ teaspoon ground cinnamon
- ½ teaspoon kosher salt
- ½ cup (1 stick) cold unsalted butter, cut into small pieces
- 1 large egg, lightly beaten

For the filling

- ½ cup (1 stick) unsalted butter
- ⅔ cup firmly packed light brown sugar
- ¼ cup light corn syrup
- ¼ cup heavy cream
- ½ teaspoon kosher salt
- 2 cups pecan halves

INSTRUCTIONS

1. Line bottom of a 9-inch-square baking pan with parchment paper, letting the paper hang slightly over two sides.

2. To make the crust, in a food processor, mix flour, granulated sugar, cinnamon and salt and pulse until combined. Add butter and pulse until mixture is coarse and crumbly. Add egg and pulse until dough comes together. Spread dough evenly into prepared pan, pressing it firmly. Using the tines of a fork, prick dough in even rows all over. Freeze until firm, about 15 minutes.

3. While dough is chilling, preheat oven to 375°F. Bake crust until light

golden brown, 20 to 25 minutes. Cool in the pan on a wire rack.

4. To make the filling, combine butter, brown sugar and corn syrup in a medium saucepan set on the stovetop over medium-high heat. Bring to a boil, whisking constantly until smooth. Continue boiling, without stirring, until slightly darkened, about 2 minutes longer. Remove pan from heat. Whisk in heavy cream and salt (be careful to avoid caramel splattering). Using a rubber spatula, fold in pecans.

quick tip
Prebaking the crust before adding the thick pecan filling keeps it from getting soggy.

5. Pour filling into crust and smooth the top with rubber spatula. Bake until bubbling, 15 to 20 minutes. Cool completely in pan on wire rack. Using parchment paper as handles, remove from pan and cut into bars.

NOTE Store bars in an airtight container at room temperature for up to 5 days.

Bar Cookies

quick tip

For easy cleanup, put the candy canes or peppermint candies in a zip-close plastic bag, then crush them with a rolling pin or meat pounder.

PEPPERMINT BARK BROWNIES

Sugar Cookie Bars

Easy • Family Favorite • Gift Idea
Nut-Free

This version of a popular holiday cookie bakes like a cake in a large pan, making plenty of bars for sharing and gifting. Choose your favorite color for the frosting, and have fun with it!

PREP 15 minutes
BAKE 30 minutes
MAKES 24 bars

INGREDIENTS

- 2¾ cups all-purpose flour
- 1 teaspoon kosher salt
- 1 cup (2 sticks) unsalted butter, at room temperature
- 1 (8-ounce) package cream cheese, at room temperature
- 1½ cups sugar
- 1 large egg
- 2 teaspoons vanilla extract
  Vanilla Frosting (page 122)
  Gel food coloring

INSTRUCTIONS

1. Preheat oven to 350°F. Coat a 13x9-inch baking pan with nonstick cooking spray or butter and line with parchment paper, letting the paper hang slightly over the ends. Spray or butter the parchment.

2. In a medium bowl, whisk together flour and salt.

3. In a large bowl, using an electric mixer, beat butter and cream cheese together on medium-high speed until well blended, 1 minute. Add sugar and beat until smooth. Add egg and vanilla extract and beat until combined. Scrape down the sides of the bowl with a rubber spatula. Add flour mixture; beat on low speed just until combined. Press dough into bottom of pan.

4. Bake until edges are light golden brown, about 30 minutes. Cool completely on wire rack.

5. While the bars cool, make the frosting. Add 1 teaspoon food coloring of your choice and mix until combined, adding more, if needed, until desired color is achieved.

6. Using parchment paper as handles, remove cookie from pan. Using a rubber or offset spatula, spread frosting on top and decorate with sprinkles. Cut into squares.

Peppermint Bark Brownies

Family Favorite • Gift Idea
Nut-Free

Fudgy brownies are topped with the quintessential holiday candy. Lining the baking pan with parchment makes it easy to remove the brownies.

PREP 15 minutes
BAKE 25 to 35 minutes
MAKES 24 bars

INGREDIENTS

For the brownies

- 4 ounces unsweetened chocolate, chopped
- 4 ounces bittersweet chocolate, chopped
- 1¼ cups (2½ sticks) unsalted butter, cut into pieces
- 1½ cups all-purpose flour
- ⅓ cup unsweetened cocoa powder
- 1 teaspoon baking powder
- 1 teaspoon kosher salt
- 5 large eggs
- 2½ cups sugar
- 2 teaspoons vanilla extract

For the topping

- 4 ounces semisweet chocolate, melted

- 1 teaspoon peppermint extract, divided
- 4 ounces white chocolate, melted
  Peppermint candies or candy canes, crushed

INSTRUCTIONS

1. Preheat oven to 350°F. Coat a 13x9-inch baking pan with nonstick cooking spray or butter and line with parchment paper, letting the paper hang slightly over two sides. Spray or butter the parchment.

2. In a medium saucepan set on the stovetop over low heat, combine unsweetened and bittersweet chocolates and butter and stir until melted. Set aside to cool slightly.

3. In a medium bowl, whisk together flour, cocoa powder, baking powder and salt.

4. In a large bowl, whisk eggs until smooth. Add sugar and vanilla and whisk until combined. Add melted chocolate mixture and whisk until combined. Using a rubber spatula, fold in flour mixture just until combined. Pour into prepared pan.

5. Bake until toothpick inserted into center of brownies comes out with moist crumbs, 25 to 35 minutes. Cool completely on wire rack. Using parchment paper as handles, remove brownies from pan.

6. In a small bowl, mix semisweet chocolate with ½ teaspoon peppermint extract. In another small bowl, mix white chocolate with ½ teaspoon peppermint extract. Using a rubber or offset spatula, spread semisweet chocolate evenly over brownies. Let set until hardened. Using a spoon, drizzle white chocolate on top. Sprinkle with crushed peppermint candies. Let set until hardened, then cut into bars.

Lemon Bars
Classic • Family Favorite • Nut-Free

Get more juice out of lemons by rolling on the counter first. You'll need 2 to 3 lemons for these bars.

PREP 15 minutes
CHILL 15 minutes
BAKE 45 to 55 minutes, in two parts
MAKES 16 bars

INGREDIENTS
For the crust
- 1⅓ cups all-purpose flour
  Pinch of kosher salt
- 10 tablespoons unsalted butter, at room temperature
- ⅓ cup granulated sugar

For the filling
- 4 large eggs
- 2½ cups granulated sugar
- 1 tablespoon freshly grated lemon zest
- ½ cup fresh lemon juice
- ⅔ cup flour
  Confectioners' sugar, for dusting

INSTRUCTIONS
1. Preheat oven to 350°F.
2. To make the crust, in a small bowl, whisk together flour and salt.
3. In a large bowl, using an electric mixer, beat butter and sugar together on medium-high speed until light and fluffy, about 2 minutes. Add flour mixture and beat on low speed just until combined. Press dough evenly into bottom of 9-inch-square baking pan. Using tines of a fork, prick dough in even rows all over. Refrigerate for 15 minutes.
4. Bake until light golden brown, 15 to 20 minutes. Cool in pan on wire rack for 15 minutes.
5. To make the filling, in a large bowl, whisk together eggs, sugar, lemon zest, lemon juice and flour. Pour over crust.
6. Bake until set, 30 to 35 minutes. Cool completely in pan on wire rack, then dust with confectioners' sugar and cut into bars.

Fudgy Brownies
Easy • Family Favorite • Nut-Free

It's better to slightly underbake brownies than to overbake them—they will continue to set as they cool down. Batter baked in metal pans will cook more quickly than those in glass, so be sure to adjust the cooking time accordingly.

PREP 15 minutes
BAKE 25 to 35 minutes
MAKES 24 bars

INGREDIENTS

- 4 ounces unsweetened chocolate, chopped
- 4 ounces semisweet or bittersweet chocolate, chopped
- 1¼ cups (2½ sticks) unsalted butter, cut into pieces
- 1½ cups all-purpose flour
- ⅓ cup unsweetened cocoa powder
- 1 teaspoon baking powder
- 1 teaspoon kosher salt
- 5 large eggs
- 2½ cups sugar
- 2 teaspoons vanilla extract

INSTRUCTIONS

1. Preheat oven to 350°F. Coat a 13x9-inch baking pan with nonstick cooking spray or butter.

2. In a medium saucepan set on the stovetop over low heat, combine both chocolates and butter and stir until melted. Set aside to cool slightly.

3. In a medium bowl, whisk together flour, cocoa powder, baking powder and salt.

4. In a large bowl, whisk eggs until smooth. Add sugar and vanilla and whisk until combined. Add melted chocolate mixture and whisk until combined. Using a rubber spatula, fold in flour mixture just until combined. Pour into prepared pan.

5. Bake until toothpick inserted into center of brownies comes out with moist crumbs, 25 to 35 minutes. Cool completely in pan on wire rack, then cut into bars.

quick tip

For an extra kick, add a shot of brewed espresso to the melted chocolate mixture—it will enhance the flavor of the chocolate in the brownies.

EVERYTHING
BARS

Chocolate-Mint Brownies

Easy • Gift Idea • Nut-Free

Hiding a peppermint patty candy inside brownie batter creates a fun surprise in every bite.

PREP 15 minutes
BAKE 25 to 35 minutes
MAKES 24 bars

INGREDIENTS

- 4 ounces unsweetened chocolate, chopped
- 4 ounces semisweet or bittersweet chocolate, chopped
- 1¼ cups (2½ sticks) unsalted butter, cut into pieces
- 1½ cups all-purpose flour
- ⅓ cup unsweetened cocoa powder
- 1 teaspoon baking powder
- 1 teaspoon kosher salt
- 5 large eggs
- 2½ cups sugar
- 2 teaspoons vanilla extract
- 24 peppermint patty candies

INSTRUCTIONS

1. Preheat oven to 350°F. Coat a 13x9-inch baking pan with nonstick cooking spray or butter.
2. In medium saucepan set on stovetop over low heat, combine both chocolates and butter and stir until melted. Set aside to cool slightly.
3. In a medium bowl, whisk together flour, cocoa powder, baking powder and salt.
4. In a large bowl, whisk eggs until smooth. Add sugar and vanilla and whisk until combined. Add melted chocolate mixture and whisk until combined. Using a rubber spatula, fold in flour mixture just until incorporated.
5. Pour half the batter into the prepared pan. Place peppermint patty candies in a single layer on top, leaving a 1-inch border from the edges of the pan. Pour remaining batter on top.

6. Bake until toothpick inserted into center of brownies comes out with moist crumbs, 25 to 35 minutes. Cool in pan on wire rack completely, then cut into bars.

Everything Bars

Classic • Easy • Family Favorite

Crush graham crackers in a food processor or in a zip-close plastic bag using a rolling pin.

PREP 10 minutes
BAKE 20 to 25 minutes
MAKES 24 bars

INGREDIENTS

- ½ cup (1 stick) unsalted butter, melted
- 10 graham crackers, crushed into crumbs
- ¾ cup semisweet or bittersweet chocolate chips
- 1 cup peanut butter chips or butterscotch chips
- ¾ cup white chocolate chips

- 1 cup old-fashioned rolled oats
- 1 cup toasted pecans, chopped
- 1 (14-ounce) can sweetened condensed milk
- 1 cup shredded coconut (sweetened or unsweetened)

INSTRUCTIONS

1. Preheat oven to 350°F. Spread melted butter evenly over bottom of a 13x9-inch baking pan.

2. Spread the graham cracker crumbs evenly over the bottom of the buttered pan. Layer the chocolate chips, peanut butter chips, white chocolate chips, oats and pecans on top. Pour milk evenly over layers. Sprinkle coconut evenly over top.

3. Bake until edges are golden and coconut is toasted, 20 to 25 minutes. Cool completely in baking pan on wire rack, then cut into bars.

MILLIONAIRE'S SHORTBREAD

Millionaire's Shortbread

Gift Idea • Nut-Free

This version of these mysteriously named bars features salted caramel in between layers of dark chocolate and shortbread.

PREP	20 minutes
CHILL	45 to 65 minutes, in two parts
BAKE	35 to 45 minutes
MAKES	16 bars

INGREDIENTS

For the crust
- 1½ cups all-purpose flour
- 1 teaspoon kosher salt
- 1 cup (2 sticks) unsalted butter, at room temperature
- ⅓ cup firmly packed light brown sugar
- ⅓ cup granulated sugar
- 1 large egg yolk
- 1 teaspoon vanilla extract

For the salted caramel filling
- ¾ cup (1½ sticks) unsalted butter, at room temperature
- ¾ cup firmly packed light brown sugar
- 1 (14 ounce) can sweetened condensed milk
- 1 teaspoon kosher salt
- 8 ounces semisweet chocolate, melted
- Flaky sea salt, for sprinkling

INSTRUCTIONS

1. Preheat oven to 300°F. Coat a 9-inch-square baking pan with nonstick cooking spray or butter and line with parchment paper, letting the paper hang slightly over two sides. Spray or butter the parchment.

2. To make the crust, in a small bowl, whisk together flour and salt.

3. In a large bowl, using an electric mixer, beat butter and both sugars together on medium-high speed until light and fluffy, about 3 minutes. Add egg yolk and vanilla and beat until combined. Scrape down the sides of the bowl with a rubber spatula. Add flour mixture and beat on low speed just until combined. Press dough into bottom of prepared pan.

4. Bake until edges are light golden brown, 35 to 45 minutes. Cool completely on wire rack.

5. To make the filling, in a medium saucepan set on the stovetop over medium-low heat, combine butter and sugar. Cook, stirring occasionally, until melted. Add condensed milk and salt and bring to a boil, stirring constantly (be careful to avoid caramel splattering), then boil for 1 minute longer without stirring. Remove pan from heat; carefully pour filling over shortbread. Let cool at room temperature for 10 minutes, then refrigerate until set, 30 to 45 minutes.

6. Pour melted chocolate over caramel and sprinkle with sea salt. Refrigerate until set, 15 to 20 minutes. Using parchment paper as handles, remove from pan and cut into bars.

Chapter 4

Specialty Cookies

INTERESTING SHAPES, FLAVORS AND TEXTURES
HELP THESE DELICACIES STAND OUT.

**RUSSIAN
TEA CAKES**

Jam Pinwheels
Gift Idea • Nut-Free

Use any flavor jam inside these soft spirals— raspberry, strawberry and other red-hued jams will look the most festive.

PREP 20 minutes
CHILL 1 hour 30 minutes
BAKE 12 to 14 minutes per batch
MAKES 4 dozen cookies

INGREDIENTS

- 3 cups all-purpose flour, plus more for dusting
- 1 teaspoon baking powder
- ½ teaspoon kosher salt
- 1 cup (2 sticks) unsalted butter, at room temperature
- 1¼ cups sugar
- 1 large egg
- 2 teaspoons vanilla extract
- 2 tablespoons whole milk
- ½ cup raspberry, strawberry or another red jam

INSTRUCTIONS

1. In a medium bowl, whisk together flour, baking powder and salt.

2. In a large bowl, using an electric mixer, beat butter and sugar together on medium-high speed until light and fluffy, about 2 minutes. Add egg and vanilla and beat until combined. Scrape down the sides of the bowl with a rubber spatula. Add flour mixture, 1 cup at a time, and milk and beat on low speed just until combined. Divide dough in half and place each half on a sheet of parchment paper.

3. Lightly flour each piece of dough and roll into a ½-inch-thick rectangle. Trim each piece of dough to a 10x8-inch rectangle. Place dough on parchment on a baking sheet (stack, if needed) and refrigerate until firm, about 1 hour.

4. Let dough sit at room temperature until soft enough to bend without cracking, 5 to 10 minutes. Using a spoon or offset spatula, spread ¼ cup jam on each rectangle, leaving a 1-inch border on the long sides and a ½-inch border on the short sides. Starting with a long side, tightly roll up dough into a log, using parchment to help you roll. Press to seal long edge of log. Cover and refrigerate until firm, about 30 minutes.

5. Preheat oven to 350°F. Line 2 baking sheets with parchment paper.

6. Working with 1 log a time, use a sharp knife to cut each log crosswise into ¼-inch-thick rounds (trim and discard rough edges). Place rounds 1 inch apart on prepared baking sheets. Bake, 1 sheet at a time, 12 to 14 minutes, or until set and edges are light golden brown, rotating sheets halfway through. Cool on baking sheets 5 minutes. Transfer cookies to wire racks to cool completely.

Russian Tea Cakes
Company-Worthy • Easy • Gift Idea

Delicate walnut cookies are covered in two layers of confectioners' sugar.

PREP 10 minutes
BAKE 15 minutes
MAKES 2½ dozen cookies

INGREDIENTS

- 2 cups walnuts
- 2 cups all-purpose flour
- 1 cup unsalted butter, at room temperature
- 6 tablespoons granulated sugar
- 1 teaspoon vanilla extract
- 1 cup confectioners' sugar

INSTRUCTIONS

1. Preheat oven to 350°F. Line 2 baking sheets with parchment paper.

2. In a food processor, grind walnuts until fine, making sure no big chunks remain. Transfer to a medium bowl. Add flour and whisk to combine.

3. In a large bowl, using an electric mixer, beat butter and granulated sugar on medium-high speed until creamy. Add vanilla and beat until combined. Add flour mixture and beat on low speed until dough starts to come together.

4. Scoop rounded tablespoons of dough (or use an ice cream scoop 1½ inches in diameter) and gently roll into balls. Place balls 2 inches apart onto prepared baking sheets. Bake, one sheet at a time, about 15 minutes or until set and light golden brown. Cool on baking sheets 5 minutes. Carefully coat each cookie in confectioners' sugar (the warm cookies crumble easily). Transfer cookies to wire cooling racks to cool completely. Coat again in confectioners' sugar.

NOTE You can store these cookies in an airtight container between layers of wax or parchment paper at room temperature for up to 1 week.

quick tip
Roll cookies in confectioners' sugar immediately after baking so the heat helps it stick, then coat them again after they've cooled.

Peppermint Meringues

Company-Worthy • Nut-Free

Egg whites whip best at room temperature. Make sure your bowl is very clean.

PREP 25 minutes
REST 30 minutes
BAKE 25 to 30 minutes per batch
MAKES 2 dozen cookies

INGREDIENTS

- 4 large egg whites, at room temperature
- 1 teaspoon kosher salt
- 2 cups confectioners' sugar
- 1 teaspoon peppermint extract
- Red gel food coloring

INSTRUCTIONS

1. Line 2 baking sheets with parchment paper.

2. In a large bowl, using an electric mixer, beat egg whites on medium-high speed until foamy, about 1 minute. Add salt and beat until foam thickens, about 1 minute. With the mixer running, gradually add the sugar, about 2 tablespoons at a time, and beat until eggs are glossy and very fluffy, about 15 minutes. Add peppermint extract and beat until it is just combined.

3. Fit a pastry bag with a star tip (we used Ateco 852). Using a thin paintbrush, paint 4 long vertical stripes of red food coloring against the insides of the pastry bag, spacing them evenly apart. Carefully spoon meringue into bag, taking care not to smear the red stripes and filling the bag no more than ¾ full.

4. Pipe meringue in a circular motion onto prepared baking sheets, creating circles about 2 inches in diameter. Refill piping bag with any remaining meringue, adding more food coloring stripes, if needed. Let stand at room temperature, uncovered, for 30 minutes.

5. Preheat oven to 250°F. Bake, 1 sheet at a time, until dry and firm to the touch, 25 to 30 minutes. Cool completely on sheets on wire racks.

NOTE Store meringues between layers of parchment paper in an airtight container at room temperature for up to 3 days.

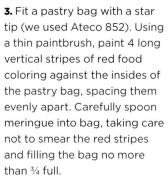
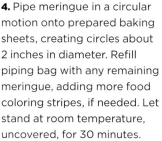

King Haakon's "Coffee Cake" Cookies

Classic • Company-Worthy
Nut-Free

A Norwegian Christmas tradition, these simple cookies are ideal with coffee or tea. Keep an eye on them while broiling so they don't burn.

PREP 20 minutes
BAKE 15 minutes, plus 2 to 3 minutes under the broiler
MAKES about 5 dozen cookies

INGREDIENTS

- 3¾ cups all-purpose flour
- 3 teaspoons baking powder
- ¾ teaspoon ground cardamom
- ¼ teaspoon ground cinnamon
  Pinch of kosher salt
- 4 large eggs
- ¾ cup sugar
- 10 tablespoons unsalted butter, melted

INSTRUCTIONS

1. Preheat oven to 375°F. Line 2 baking sheets with parchment paper.

2. In a medium bowl, whisk together flour, baking powder, cardamom, cinnamon and salt.

3. In a large bowl, using an electric mixer, beat eggs on medium-high speed until foamy, about 2 minutes. Add sugar and beat until combined. Add melted butter and beat until combined. Add flour mixture and beat on low speed until dough comes together.

4. Divide dough into 4 pieces. Roll each into a log about 1½ inches in diameter. Place logs on prepared baking sheets, 2 per sheet, and bake until tops are lightly browned, about 15 minutes.

5. Preheat the broiler. While logs are still warm, cut each into ½-inch-thick slices. Remove parchment paper from baking sheets. Place slices 2 inches apart on unlined baking sheets. Broil for 1½ minutes, flip cookies, and broil for 1½ to 2 minutes longer, until edges are golden but centers are pale and still slightly soft. Cool on baking sheets, 1 to 2 minutes. Transfer to wire racks and let cool completely.

NOTE Freeze cookies in a freezer-safe zip-close bag for up to 1 month.

quick tip
A quick second bake under the broiler creates crispy edges without drying out the cookies.

Madeleines
Classic • Easy • Nut-Free

You'll need a madeleine pan for these iconic French cookies, which are best eaten warm. Chilling the dough before baking makes piping and filling the molds much easier.

PREP   10 minutes
CHILL   30 to 60 minutes
BAKE   5 to 7 minutes per batch
MAKES   about 2 dozen cookies

INGREDIENTS
- 1 cup all-purpose flour, plus more for the pan
- ⅔ cup sugar
- ½ teaspoon baking powder
- 2 teaspoons freshly grated lemon zest
- Pinch of kosher salt
- 2 large eggs, lightly beaten
- ½ cup (1 stick) unsalted butter, melted
- Confectioners' sugar, for serving

INSTRUCTIONS
1. In a large bowl, whisk together flour, sugar, baking powder, lemon zest and salt. Add eggs and gently whisk to combine. Slowly stir in melted butter with a rubber spatula just until combined. Cover with plastic wrap and refrigerate until firm, 30 to 60 minutes.

2. Preheat oven to 400°F. Butter and flour a madeleine pan.

3. Fit a pastry bag with a large round piping tip. Pipe batter into molds, filling each ¾ full.

4. Bake until cookies are puffed up and edges are light golden brown, 5 to 7 minutes. Cool in pan 5 minutes; invert pan and unmold cookies. Sprinkle with confectioners' sugar and serve warm. Repeat to bake remaining batter (wash, re-butter and re-flour pan between batches).

Spiral Cookies

Family Favorite • Gift Idea
Nut-Free

Divide cookie dough and tint one half with red gel food coloring to create these festive spirals.

PREP 20 minutes
CHILL 1 hour 30 minutes
BAKE 12 to 14 minutes per batch
MAKES 3 dozen cookies

INGREDIENTS

- 3 cups all-purpose flour, plus more for dusting
- 1 teaspoon baking powder
- ½ teaspoon kosher salt
- 1 cup (2 sticks) unsalted butter, at room temperature
- 1¼ cups sugar
- 1 large egg, lightly beaten
- 2 teaspoons vanilla extract
- 2 tablespoons whole milk
- Red gel food coloring
- 1 large egg white, lightly beaten

INSTRUCTIONS

1. In a medium bowl, whisk together flour, baking powder and salt.

2. In a large bowl, using an electric mixer, beat butter and sugar together on medium-high speed until light and fluffy, about 2 minutes. Add whole egg and vanilla and beat until combined. Scrape down the sides of the bowl with a rubber spatula. Add flour mixture, 1 cup at a time, and milk and beat on low speed just until combined. Place half the dough on a sheet of parchment paper. Add ½ teaspoon red food coloring to the remaining dough in the bowl and beat on low speed just until all the coloring is absorbed. Add more coloring, if needed, until desired color is achieved. Place red dough on a separate sheet of parchment paper.

3. Lightly flour each piece of dough and roll into a ¼-inch-thick rectangle. Trim each piece of dough to a 12x10-inch rectangle. Place dough on parchment on a baking sheet (stack, if needed) and refrigerate until firm, about 1 hour.

4. Brush egg white on top of each rectangle. Remove parchment paper from white dough and place white dough on top of red dough. Starting with a long side, tightly roll up dough into a log, using parchment to help you roll. Seal the long edge of the log with egg white. Cover and refrigerate until firm, about 30 minutes.

5. Preheat the oven to 350°F. Line 2 baking sheets with parchment paper.

6. Using a sharp knife, cut log crosswise into ¼-inch-thick rounds (trim and discard rough edges). Place rounds 1 inch apart on prepared baking sheets. Bake, 1 sheet at a time, 12 to 14 minutes, or until set but not browned, rotating sheets halfway through. Cool on baking sheets 5 minutes. Transfer cookies to wire racks to cool completely.

quick tip

You can tint half the dough red and the other half green to create a very festive spiral cookie.

Chapter 5

Layers and Bundts

CHOCOLATE, PEPPERMINT, GINGER AND MORE
SPICE UP THESE SHOWSTOPPING CAKES.

CHOCOLATE-MINT
BUNDT CAKE
WITH CHOCOLATE
GANACHE, PAGE 69

quick tip
Use full-fat coconut milk for the best flavor and to keep the cake moist.

COCONUT-CHOCOLATE LAYER CAKE

Coconut-Chocolate Layer Cake

Easy • Family Favorite • Nut-Free

Toasting coconut enhances its flavor and texture. Use a vegetable peeler to make chocolate shavings from a bar of milk or dark chocolate.

PREP 15 minutes
BAKE 25 to 30 minutes
MAKES 8 to 10 servings

INGREDIENTS

- 1 cup sweetened, shredded coconut
- 1 cup coconut milk
- 3 large eggs
- 1 teaspoon vanilla extract
- 1 teaspoon almond extract
- 2¼ cups all-purpose flour, plus more for dusting
- 1½ cups sugar
- 3 teaspoons baking powder
- 1 teaspoon kosher salt
- 1 cup (2 sticks) unsalted butter, at room temperature, cut into cubes
  Chocolate Frosting (page 121)
  Chocolate shavings, for decorating (optional)

INSTRUCTIONS

1. Preheat oven to 325°F. Coat two 8-inch round cake pans with nonstick cooking spray or butter and dust with flour, or line with parchment paper.

2. Line a baking sheet with parchment paper. Spread shredded coconut evenly across the prepared baking sheet and toast until light brown, 3 to 4 minutes. Cool on wire rack while you make the cake.

3. In a medium bowl, whisk together coconut milk, eggs, vanilla and almond extracts.

4. In a large bowl, whisk together flour, sugar, baking powder and salt. Using a rubber spatula, fold in the toasted coconut. Using an electric mixer, beat in butter on low speed until crumbly, about 1 minute. Add coconut milk mixture and beat until combined, 1 minute. Divide batter evenly between prepared cake pans.

5. Bake until a toothpick inserted into the center of cake comes out clean and top is light golden brown, 25 to 30 minutes. Cool on wire rack for 10 minutes, then transfer cakes directly to rack to cool completely.

6. While the cakes cool, make the frosting.

7. To assemble the cake, place one layer, rounded-side down, on a large plate or serving platter. Spread ⅓ of frosting evenly over top. Place second layer, rounded-side down, on top. Spread remaining frosting evenly over top and sides of cake. Sprinkle with chocolate shavings, if desired.

Chocolate-Mint Bundt Cake With Chocolate Ganache

Company-Worthy • Easy • Nut-Free

You can leave out the peppermint extract for a quick and easy chocolate cake that's delicious any time of the year.

PREP 10 minutes
BAKE 40 minutes
MAKES 8 to 10 servings

INGREDIENTS

- 2 cups all-purpose flour
- 2 cups sugar
- ¾ cup unsweetened cocoa powder
- 2 teaspoons baking soda
- 1 teaspoon baking powder
- 1 teaspoon kosher salt
- 1 cup buttermilk
- ½ cup canola or vegetable oil
- 2 large eggs
- 1 teaspoon peppermint extract
- 1 teaspoon vanilla extract
  Chocolate Ganache (page 125)
  Chopped red-and-white striped peppermint candies (optional)

INSTRUCTIONS

1. Preheat oven to 350°F. Coat a 10-inch Bundt pan with nonstick cooking spray.

2. In a large bowl, whisk together flour, sugar, cocoa powder, baking soda, baking powder and salt.

3. In a medium bowl, whisk together buttermilk, oil, eggs, peppermint and vanilla extracts. Using an electric mixer, slowly beat the wet ingredients into the dry ingredients just until combined. Pour batter into prepared pan.

4. Bake until a toothpick inserted in the center of the cake comes out clean, about 40 minutes. Cool pan on wire rack for 30 minutes, then transfer cake to rack to cool completely.

5. While the cake is cooling, make the chocolate ganache. Line a baking sheet with parchment paper or aluminum foil. Set a wire rack over the baking sheet. Pour the cooled ganache evenly over the top of cake, letting it drip down the sides. Sprinkle the top with chopped peppermint candies, if using. Let ganache set 20 to 30 minutes before serving.

Spice Cake With Orange Frosting
Easy • Family Favorite • Nut-Free

Citrus and spice are a classic flavor combination that will get you in the holiday spirit.

PREP 25 minutes
BAKE 20 to 25 minutes
MAKES 10 to 12 servings

INGREDIENTS

- 1 cup unsulfured molasses
- 1 cup boiling water
- 4 cups all-purpose flour
- 1 tablespoon baking soda
- 1 tablespoon ground ginger
- 1 tablespoon ground cinnamon
- 1 teaspoon ground nutmeg
- 1 teaspoon ground allspice
- ¼ teaspoon ground cloves
- 1 teaspoon kosher salt
- 1 cup (2 sticks) unsalted butter, at room temperature
- 1 cup firmly packed light brown sugar
- 1 tablespoon freshly grated orange zest (from about 1 orange)
- 4 large eggs
  Orange Frosting (page 122)

INSTRUCTIONS

1. Preheat oven to 350°F. Coat three 9-inch round cake pans with butter or nonstick cooking spray and line with parchment paper.

2. In a medium bowl, stir together molasses and water. Set aside.

3. In another medium bowl, whisk flour, baking soda, ginger, cinnamon, nutmeg, allspice, cloves and salt.

4. In a large bowl, using an electric mixer, beat butter, sugar and orange zest together on medium-high speed until light and fluffy, about 2 minutes. Add eggs, one at a time, and beat until well combined. Add flour mixture in three parts, alternating with the molasses mixture, beating on low speed until combined and scraping down the sides of the bowl with a rubber spatula after each addition. Divide batter evenly among prepared pans and spread top with an offset spatula or butter knife.

5. Bake until toothpick inserted into center of cake comes out clean, 20 to 25 minutes. Cool on wire racks for 10 minutes, then transfer cakes directly to racks to cool completely.

6. While the cakes cool, make the frosting.

7. To assemble the cake, place one layer, rounded-side down, on a large plate or serving platter. Spread ⅓ of frosting evenly over top. Place second layer, rounded-side down, on top. Spread ⅓ of frosting evenly over top. Repeat with third layer, spreading remaining frosting evenly over top and sides of cake.

Christmas Present Cake
Family Favorite • Nut-Free

Red fruit leather creates a ribbon effect on a cake that would look right at home under the tree.

PREP 15 minutes
BAKE 25 to 30 minutes
MAKES 8 to 10 servings

INGREDIENTS

  2   cups all-purpose flour
  2   cups sugar
  ¾   cup unsweetened
      cocoa powder
  2   teaspoons baking soda
  1   teaspoon baking powder
  1   teaspoon kosher salt
  1   cup buttermilk
  ½   cup canola or vegetable oil
  2   large eggs
  1   teaspoon vanilla extract
      Vanilla Frosting (page 122)
      Raspberry or strawberry fruit
      leather (like Roll-Ups)

INSTRUCTIONS

1. Preheat oven to 350°F. Coat two 8-inch-square cake pans with butter or nonstick cooking spray.

2. In a large bowl, whisk together flour, sugar, cocoa powder, baking soda, baking powder and salt.

3. In a medium bowl, whisk together buttermilk, oil, eggs and vanilla. Using an electric mixer, slowly beat the wet ingredients into the dry ingredients just until combined. Divide batter evenly between prepared pans.

4. Bake until a toothpick inserted in the center of the cake comes out clean, 25 to 30 minutes. Cool pans on wire racks for 30 minutes, then transfer cakes directly to rack to cool completely.

5. While the cake is baking, make the frosting.

6. To assemble cake, place one layer, rounded side down, on a large plate. Spread ⅓ of frosting evenly over top. Place second layer, rounded side down, on top. Spread remaining frosting evenly over top and sides of cake as desired.

7. To make a ribbon using the fruit leather, starting in the center at the bottom of one side of the cake, place a fruit-leather strip up the side of the cake, across the top, and down the other side of the cake. (If your strips are not long enough to cover the entire cake, you can overlap two strips.) Repeat on the adjacent side of the cake. Twist another strip into a bow shape and place it on the top of the cake.

Apple Spice Bundt Cake
Easy • Nut-Free

Tart, always-in-season apples, such as Granny Smith, balance the sweetness of this moist, flavorful cake, and make it easy to bake year-round.

PREP 15 minutes
BAKE 70 to 80 minutes
MAKES 8 to 10 servings

INGREDIENTS
- 3 cups all-purpose flour, plus more for dusting
- 1 tablespoon ground cinnamon
- ¼ teaspoon ground nutmeg
- ¼ teaspoon ground cloves
- 1 teaspoon baking soda
- 1 teaspoon kosher salt
- 1 cup canola or vegetable oil
- 3 large eggs
- 1½ cups sugar
- 1 teaspoon vanilla extract
- 4 medium tart apples, such as Granny Smith, peeled, cored and cut into ½-inch pieces (about 3 cups)
  Confectioners' sugar, for dusting

INSTRUCTIONS
1. Preheat oven to 350°F. Coat a 10-inch Bundt pan with nonstick cooking spray and lightly dust with flour.

2. In a medium bowl, whisk together flour, cinnamon, nutmeg, cloves, baking soda and salt.

3. In a large bowl, using an electric mixer, beat oil, eggs, sugar and vanilla together on medium speed until combined. Add flour mixture and beat on low speed just until combined. Using a rubber spatula, fold in the apples. Pour batter into prepared pan.

4. Bake until a toothpick inserted in the center of the cake comes out clean, 70 to 80 minutes. Cool in pan on wire rack for 30 minutes, then transfer cake to rack to cool completely. Sprinkle with confectioners' sugar.

quick tip
For a luxurious finish, drizzle this cake with Brown-Butter Glaze (page 122) instead of dusting it with confectioners' sugar.

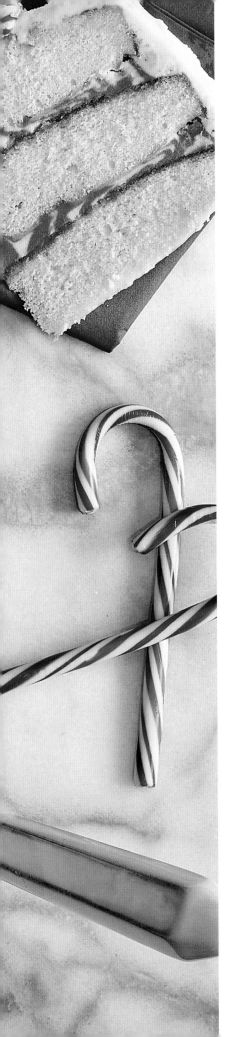

Candy Cane Layer Cake

Family Favorite • Nut-Free

Place candy canes or peppermints in a zip-close bag, and crush with a rolling pin or meat pounder. Be careful not to turn all into powder, you want a few bigger chunks.

PREP 15 minutes
BAKE 20 minutes
MAKES 10 to 12 servings

INGREDIENTS

- 2 cups cake flour
- 1 cup all-purpose flour
- 2 cups sugar
- 1 tablespoon baking powder
- 1 teaspoon kosher salt
- 1 cup (2 sticks) unsalted butter, cut into small cubes
- 4 large eggs
- 1 cup whole milk
- 1 teaspoon peppermint extract
- 1 teaspoon vanilla extract
  Vanilla Frosting (page 122)
- 1 teaspoon red gel food coloring, plus more as desired
  Crushed candy canes or peppermint candies, for decorating

INSTRUCTIONS

1. Preheat oven to 350°F. Coat three 9-inch round cake pans with butter or nonstick cooking spray and line with parchment paper.

2. In a large bowl or the bowl of a stand mixer, whisk together flours, sugar, baking powder and salt. Using an electric mixer, beat in butter cubes on low speed just until coated.

3. In a medium bowl or large measuring cup, whisk together eggs, milk, peppermint and vanilla extracts. With mixer on low speed, add wet ingredients to flour mixture and beat until combined. Do not overmix. Divide batter evenly among prepared pans.

4. Bake until light golden brown and a toothpick inserted in center of cake comes out clean, about 20 minutes, rotating pans halfway through so they bake evenly. Cool on wire racks for 10 minutes, then transfer cakes directly to racks to cool completely. Remove and discard parchment.

5. While the cakes cool, make the frosting. Place ⅓ of the frosting in a medium bowl. Add red food coloring and mix well until combined, adding more, if needed, until desired color is achieved.

6. Fit a pastry bag with a large, round tip. Transfer the red frosting into the pastry bag, keeping it on one side; transfer half of the remaining white frosting to the other side of the pastry bag.

7. To assemble the cake, place one cake layer, rounded-side down, on a large plate or serving platter. Pipe ½ of the frosting in the pastry bag evenly over top— this will create a swirl effect. Place another layer, rounded-side down, gently on top. Pipe the remaining swirled frosting in the pastry bag evenly over top. Place the final layer gently on top, spreading the remaining white frosting evenly over top and sides of cake. Cover the top and bottom edge of the cake with crushed candy canes.

NOTE To easily add some decorations to the lower side edge of the cake, place strips of parchment paper underneath the cake before frosting. Place decorations all around the bottom of the cake and lift the parchment paper up, gently using it to press the decorations into the frosting. Remove parchment strips just before serving.

Lemon Drizzle Bundt Cake
Family Favorite • Nut-Free

For a more subtle lemon flavor in the glaze, substitute fresh lemon juice for milk or water and omit the lemon extract.

PREP 15 minutes
BAKE 45 to 55 minutes
MAKES 8 to 10 servings

INGREDIENTS

- 2¼ cups all-purpose flour, plus more for dusting
- 1 tablespoon poppy seeds, plus more for sprinkling
- 1½ teaspoons baking powder
- ½ teaspoon kosher salt
- 1¼ cups (2½ sticks) unsalted butter, at room temperature
- 1½ cups granulated sugar
  Freshly grated zest of 1 lemon
- 3 large eggs, at room temperature
- ¾ cup sour cream
- 1 teaspoon pure vanilla extract
  5-Minute Lemon Icing (page 123)

INSTRUCTIONS

1. Preheat oven to 350°F. Coat a 10-inch Bundt pan with nonstick cooking spray and lightly dust with flour.

2. In a medium bowl, whisk together flour, poppy seeds, baking powder and salt.

3. In a large bowl, using an electric mixer, beat butter, sugar and lemon zest together on medium-high speed until fluffy, about 2 minutes. Beat in eggs. Add sour cream and vanilla and beat until combined, about 1 minute. Add flour mixture and beat on low speed until just combined. Pour batter into prepared pan.

4. Bake until toothpick inserted into center of cake comes out clean, 45 to 55 minutes. Cool in pan on wire rack for 15 minutes.

5. While cake is cooling, make the glaze. Line a baking sheet with parchment paper or foil. Remove cake from pan and return to cooling rack set over prepared baking sheet. Pour glaze evenly over top of cake, letting it drip down the sides. Sprinkle with poppy seeds. Let glaze set 15 minutes before serving.

quick tip

Decorate this boldly hued holiday cake with any type of sprinkles you like—red, green or a combination would all look festive.

Red Velvet Layer Cake

Classic • Nut-Free

Add as much of the gel food coloring as you like to this classic cake until the desired red hue is reached. Be careful, as it is more saturated— you might want to wear kitchen gloves when working with the food coloring and be sure to use a metal bowl to avoid staining your countertop or work surface.

PREP 20 minutes
BAKE 25 to 30 minutes
MAKES 8 to 10 servings

INGREDIENTS

- 1⅔ cups all-purpose flour, plus more for dusting
- 1 cup sugar
- 1 tablespoon cocoa powder
- 1 teaspoon baking soda
- ½ teaspoon kosher salt
- 1 cup canola or vegetable oil
- ⅔ cup buttermilk
- 2 large eggs
- 1 teaspoon white distilled vinegar
- 1 teaspoon vanilla extract
- 1 teaspoon red gel food coloring, plus more as desired
- Cream Cheese Frosting (page 121)

INSTRUCTIONS

1. Preheat oven to 350°F. Coat two 8-inch round cake pans with nonstick cooking spray and dust with flour or line with parchment paper.

2. In a large bowl, whisk together flour, sugar, cocoa powder, baking soda and salt. In a medium bowl, whisk together oil, buttermilk, eggs, vinegar and vanilla. Using an electric mixer, beat wet ingredients into flour mixture on medium speed just until combined, 1 minute. Add food coloring and beat until combined, adding more, if needed, until desired red color is reached.

3. Divide batter evenly between prepared pans. Bake until toothpick inserted into center of cake comes out clean, 25 to 30 minutes. Cool on wire rack for 10 minutes, then transfer cakes directly to rack to cool completely.

4. While the cakes cool, make the frosting.

5. To assemble the cake, place one layer, rounded-side down, on a large plate or serving platter. Spread ⅓ of frosting evenly over top. Place second layer, rounded-side down, on top. Spread remaining frosting evenly over top and sides of cake.

quick tip

Cake flour has a lower protein content than all purpose flour, leading to a softer, more tender and fluffier end product.

CHRISTMAS LAYER CAKE

Christmas Layer Cake
Company-Worthy • Nut-Free

You can cover just the top of this red, white and green layer cake in Christmas-colored sprinkles, or go crazy and adorn the sides with sprinkles as well.

PREP 20 minutes
BAKE 20 minutes
MAKES 10 to 12 servings

INGREDIENTS

- 2 cups cake flour
- 1 cup all-purpose flour
- 2 cups sugar
- 1 tablespoon baking powder
- 1 teaspoon kosher salt
- 1 cup (2 sticks) unsalted butter, cut into small cubes
- 4 large eggs
- 1 cup whole milk
- 1 teaspoon vanilla extract
- 1 teaspoon each red and green gel food coloring, plus more as desired
  Christmas-colored sprinkles or nonpareils
  Vanilla Frosting (page 122)

INSTRUCTIONS

1. Preheat oven to 350°F. Coat three 9-inch round cake pans with butter or nonstick cooking spray and line with parchment paper.
2. In a large bowl, whisk together flours, sugar, baking powder and salt. Using an electric mixer, beat in butter cubes on low speed just until coated.
3. In a medium bowl or large measuring cup, whisk together eggs, milk and vanilla. With the mixer on low speed, add the wet ingredients to the flour mixture and beat just until combined. Do not overmix.
4. Pour ⅓ of the batter into one of the prepared pans. Divide the remaining batter between two bowls. Add 1 teaspoon red gel food coloring to one bowl and 1 teaspoon green gel food coloring to the other bowl, adding more, if needed, until desired color is achieved. Pour red batter into one of the prepared pans and green batter into remaining pan.
5. Bake until toothpick inserted in center of cake comes out clean, about 20 minutes, rotating pans halfway through so they bake evenly. Cool in pans on wire racks for 10 minutes, then transfer cakes directly to racks to cool completely. Remove and discard parchment.
6. While the cakes cool, make the frosting.
7. To assemble the cake, place the green layer, rounded-side down, on a large plate or serving platter. Spread ⅓ of frosting evenly over top. Place the white layer, rounded-side down, on top. Spread ⅓ of frosting evenly over top. Repeat with the red layer, spreading remaining frosting evenly over top and sides of cake. Cover the top and sides completely with sprinkles. (See note, page 75, for tip on decorating sides.)

Chocolate Gingerbread Cake
Easy • Nut-Free

This light cake is filled with all the best flavors of Christmas.

PREP 25 minutes
BAKE 25 minutes
MAKES 8 to 10 servings

INGREDIENTS

- 2 teaspoons baking soda
- 11/3 cups boiling water
- 2½ cups all-purpose flour
- ½ cup unsweetened cocoa powder
- 2 teaspoons ground ginger
- 1½ teaspoons ground cinnamon
- ½ teaspoon ground nutmeg
- 1 teaspoon kosher salt
- ¾ cup (1½ sticks) unsalted butter, at room temperature
- 1 cup firmly packed dark brown sugar
- 2 large eggs
- 1 cup unsulfured molasses
  Chocolate Ganache (page 125)
  Crystallized ginger, chopped, for serving (optional)

INSTRUCTIONS

1. Preheat oven to 350°F. Coat two 8-inch round cake pans with butter or nonstick cooking spray and line with parchment paper.
2. In a small bowl, stir together baking soda and water until dissolved. Set aside.
3. In a medium bowl, whisk together flour, cocoa powder, ginger, cinnamon, nutmeg and salt.
4. In a large bowl, using an electric mixer, beat butter and sugar together on medium-high speed until light and fluffy, about 2 minutes. Scrape down the sides of the bowl with a rubber spatula. Add eggs and beat until well combined. Add half the flour mixture and beat on low speed just until combined. Add molasses and baking-soda mixture and beat until combined. Scrape down the sides of the bowl. Add remaining flour mixture and beat until well combined. Divide batter evenly between prepared pans and smooth the top with an offset spatula or butter knife.
5. Bake until toothpick inserted in center of cake comes out clean, about 25 minutes. Cool in pan on wire rack for 15 minutes, then transfer cakes directly to rack to cool completely. Remove and discard the parchment.
6. While cakes are cooling, make the ganache. Place one cake layer, rounded-side down, on a large plate or serving platter. Coat evenly with ganache. Top with second cake layer, rounded-side down, and spread ganache evenly over top and sides of cake. Decorate with ginger, if using. Let ganache set 30 minutes before serving.

Gingerbread Bundt Cake With Brown-Butter Glaze

Easy • Family Favorite • Nut-Free

Lots of spices flavor this holiday cake, which can also be baked in two 9x5-inch loaf pans instead of one Bundt pan.

PREP 15 minutes

BAKE 45 to 50 minutes

MAKES 8 to 10 servings

INGREDIENTS

- 3 cups all-purpose flour, plus more for dusting
- 1 teaspoon baking soda
- 2½ tablespoons ground ginger
- 1½ teaspoons ground cinnamon
- ½ teaspoon ground cloves
- ½ teaspoon ground nutmeg
- ½ teaspoon kosher salt
- 1 cup (2 sticks) unsalted butter, at room temperature
- 1 cup firmly packed dark brown sugar
- 1 large egg
- ¾ cup unsulfured molasses
- 1 cup buttermilk
  Brown-Butter Glaze (page 122)

INSTRUCTIONS

1. Preheat oven to 350°F. Coat a 10-inch Bundt pan with nonstick cooking spray and lightly dust with flour.

2. In a large bowl, whisk together flour, baking soda, ginger, cinnamon, cloves, nutmeg and salt.

3. In another large bowl, using an electric mixer, beat butter and sugar together on medium speed until fluffy, about 2 minutes. Beat in the egg. Add molasses and beat until combined, about 2 minutes. Add half the flour mixture and beat on low speed until just combined. Beat in the buttermilk. Add remaining flour mixture and beat until just combined. Don't overmix. Pour batter into prepared pan.

4. Bake until toothpick inserted into center of cake comes out clean, 45 to 50 minutes. Cool in pan on wire rack for 15 minutes.

5. While cake is cooling, make the glaze. Line a baking sheet with parchment paper or foil. Remove cake from pan and return to cooling rack set over prepared baking sheet. Pour glaze evenly over top of cake, letting it drip down the sides. Let glaze set for 15 minutes before serving.

"Naked" Carrot Cake
Family Favorite • Nut-Free

Leave the sides of this classic cake unfrosted to create a "naked" effect. Grate carrots into a metal bowl—they can stain ceramic surfaces.

PREP 15 minutes
BAKE 25 to 30 minutes
MAKES 8 to 10 servings

INGREDIENTS

- 2 cups all-purpose flour, plus more for dusting
- 1½ cups granulated sugar
- ½ cup firmly packed light brown sugar
- 2 teaspoons baking soda
- 1 teaspoon ground cinnamon
- 1 teaspoon ground allspice
- 1 teaspoon kosher salt
- 4 large eggs
- ¾ cup canola or vegetable oil
- ¾ cup plain, whole-milk yogurt
- 3 cups grated carrots (about 6 medium carrots)
- Cream Cheese Frosting (page 121)

INSTRUCTIONS

1. Preheat oven to 350°F. Coat three 9-inch round cake pans with nonstick cooking spray and dust with flour or line with parchment paper.

2. In a large bowl, whisk together flour, sugars, baking soda, cinnamon, allspice and salt. In a medium bowl, whisk together eggs, oil and yogurt. Using an electric mixer, beat wet ingredients into flour mixture on medium speed just until combined, 1 minute. Using a rubber spatula, fold in carrots.

3. Divide batter evenly among prepared pans. Bake until toothpick inserted into center of cake comes out clean, 25 to 30 minutes. Cool on wire racks for 10 minutes, then transfer cakes directly to racks to cool completely.

4. While the cakes cool, make the frosting. To assemble the cake, place one layer, rounded-side down, on a large plate or serving platter. Spread ⅓ of frosting evenly over top. Place second layer, rounded-side down, on top. Spread ⅓ of frosting evenly over top. Repeat with third layer, spreading remaining frosting evenly over top, leaving sides of cake "naked."

PUMPKIN-CHOCOLATE
CHIP BREAD, PAGE 85

Chapter 6

Quick Breads and Loaves

THESE TREATS COME TOGETHER IN A SNAP,
SO CHOOSE YOUR FAVORITE AND GET BAKING!

quick tip

Store leftovers of this family-size cake in an airtight container, or in the baking dish covered tightly with foil, for up to 5 days.

CHRISTMAS MORNING CRUMB CAKE

Christmas Morning Crumb Cake

Family Favorite • Make Ahead Nut-Free

You can bake this classic cake a few days ahead—the longer it rests, the more the rich, thick crumb topping melds into the cake. Finish with a dusting of confectioners' sugar or a drizzle of sweet icing before serving.

PREP 20 minutes
BAKE 50 to 60 minutes
MAKES 12 servings

INGREDIENTS

For the crumb topping
- 2½ cups all-purpose flour
- 1½ cups firmly packed dark brown sugar
- 1 tablespoon ground cinnamon
- ½ teaspoon kosher salt
- 1 cup (2 sticks) unsalted butter, melted
- 2 teaspoons vanilla extract

For the cake
- 3½ cups all-purpose flour
- 1 teaspoon baking powder
- ½ teaspoon baking soda
- 1 teaspoon kosher salt
- 1 cup (2 sticks) unsalted butter, at room temperature, plus more for greasing
- 1½ cups granulated sugar
- 3 large eggs
- 2 teaspoons vanilla extract
- 1½ cups sour cream or plain, full-fat Greek yogurt
  Confectioners' sugar, for dusting, or 5-Minute Icing (page 123)

INSTRUCTIONS

1. Preheat oven to 350°F. Coat a 9x12-inch baking dish with butter or nonstick cooking spray and line bottom with parchment paper.
2. To make the crumb topping, in a large bowl using a wooden spoon, mix flour, brown sugar, cinnamon, salt, butter and vanilla. Set aside.
3. To make the cake, in a medium bowl, whisk together flour, baking powder, baking soda and salt.
4. In a large bowl, using an electric mixer, beat butter and sugar together on medium-high speed until light and fluffy, about 2 minutes. Add eggs and vanilla and beat until combined. Add half the flour mixture and beat on low speed until combined. Scrape down the sides of the bowl with a rubber spatula. Add sour cream and beat until combined. Add remaining flour mixture and beat just until combined. (Batter will be thick.) Pour into prepared pan and spread evenly with an offset spatula or butter knife. Cover with crumb topping, pressing gently to adhere. (The topping layer will be thick.)
5. Bake until toothpick inserted in center of cake comes out clean and top is golden brown, 50 to 60 minutes. (Check cake after 40 minutes; if it's browning too quickly, tent with aluminum foil.) Cool in pan on wire rack for 30 minutes, then transfer cake directly to rack to cool completely. Sprinkle with confectioners' sugar or drizzle with icing, as desired.

Pumpkin-Chocolate Chip Bread

Easy • Family Favorite • Nut-Free

Irresistibly moist, this versatile quick bread is equally delicious filled with raisins or chopped nuts.

PREP 15 minutes
BAKE 1 hour
MAKES 2 loaf cakes

INGREDIENTS

- 2⅓ cups all-purpose flour
- 1 cup whole-wheat flour
- 2 cups sugar
- 2 teaspoons baking soda
- 2 teaspoons ground cinnamon
- 1½ teaspoons ground nutmeg
- 1½ teaspoons kosher salt
- ½ cup canola or vegetable oil
- 4 large eggs
- 1 cup cold water
- 2 cups canned or cooked pumpkin (not pumpkin pie filling)
- 1 (10-ounce) bag mini semisweet chocolate chips

INSTRUCTIONS

1. Preheat oven to 350°F. Coat two 9x5-inch loaf pans with nonstick cooking spray.
2. In a large bowl, whisk together both flours, sugar, baking soda, cinnamon, nutmeg and salt.
3. In another large bowl, whisk together oil, eggs, water and pumpkin. Add flour mixture to wet ingredients and mix with a wooden spoon just until combined. Fold in chocolate chips. Pour into prepared pans.
4. Bake until toothpick inserted into center of bread comes out clean, about 1 hour. (Check breads after 40 minutes; if they're browning too quickly, tent pans with aluminum foil.) Cool loaves in pan on wire rack for 30 minutes, then transfer breads directly to a wire rack to cool completely.

Pecan-Dusted Banana Bread

Classic • Easy • Family Favorite

Include the pecan "dust" that emerges when you finely chop the nuts for this topping—though you can also leave off the pecans for a nut-free bread. If you don't have whole-wheat flour on hand, you can bake entirely with all-purpose flour.

PREP   15 minutes
BAKE   50 to 60 minutes
MAKES   1 loaf cake

INGREDIENTS

- 1 cup all-purpose flour
- ½ cup whole-wheat flour
- 1 teaspoon baking soda
- 1 teaspoon salt
- ½ cup (1 stick) unsalted butter, at room temperature
- ½ cup sugar
- 2 large eggs
- 1 cup (about 2 large) very ripe mashed bananas
- ¾ cup sour cream
- 2 teaspoons vanilla extract
- ½ cup pecans, finely chopped

INSTRUCTIONS

1. Preheat oven to 350°F. Coat a 9x5-inch loaf pan with nonstick cooking spray.

2. In a large bowl, whisk together all-purpose and whole-wheat flours, baking soda and salt.

3. In another large bowl, using an electric mixer, beat butter and sugar together on medium-high speed until light and fluffy, about 2 minutes. Add eggs and beat until combined. Add flour mixture and beat on low speed just until incorporated. Add bananas, sour cream and vanilla and beat just until combined. Pour into prepared pan and sprinkle pecans on top.

4. Bake until toothpick inserted in center of bread comes out clean, 50 to 60 minutes. (Check bread after 40 minutes; if it's browning too quickly, tent with aluminum foil.) Cool in pan on wire rack for 30 minutes, then transfer bread directly to rack to cool completely.

Cranberry-Raisin Bread

Company-Worthy • Easy • Nut-Free

Use a food processor to quickly chop the cranberries. Golden raisins, aka sultanas, are smaller, sweeter and juicer than other raisins, but if you can't find them, regular brown raisins will work, too.

PREP 15 minutes
BAKE 60 to 70 minutes
MAKES 1 loaf cake

INGREDIENTS

- 2 cups all-purpose flour
- 1 cup sugar
- 1½ teaspoons baking powder
- ½ teaspoon baking soda
- 1 teaspoon kosher salt
- 4 tablespoons (½ stick) unsalted butter, cut into small pieces
- 1 egg, lightly beaten
- 1 tablespoon freshly grated orange zest (from about 1 orange)
- ¾ cup orange juice
- 1½ cups fresh or thawed, frozen cranberries, chopped
- 1 cup golden raisins

INSTRUCTIONS

1. Preheat oven to 350°F. Coat a 9x5-inch loaf pan with nonstick cooking spray.

2. In a large bowl, whisk together flour, sugar, baking powder, baking soda and salt. Add butter and use a fork to mix until crumbly. Using a wooden spoon, mix in egg, orange zest and juice just until combined. Fold in cranberries and raisins. Pour into prepared loaf pan.

3. Bake until toothpick inserted into center of bread comes out clean, 60 to 70 minutes. (Check bread after 40 minutes; if it's browning too quickly, tent with aluminum foil.) Cool in pan on wire rack for 30 minutes, then transfer bread directly to rack to cool completely.

Marble Pound Cake

Classic • Family Favorite
Make Ahead

It doesn't take much swirling to create the iconic black-and-white pattern in this traditional cake, so don't overdo it or the pattern will look muddled.

PREP 20 minutes
BAKE 40 to 50 minutes
MAKES 1 loaf

INGREDIENTS

- 2 cups cake flour
- 2 teaspoons baking powder
- 1 teaspoon kosher salt
- ½ cup (1 stick) unsalted butter, at room temperature
- 1¼ cups sugar
- 3 large eggs
- 1 teaspoon vanilla extract
- ⅔ cup buttermilk
- ¼ cup unsweetened cocoa powder
- ¼ cup boiling water

INSTRUCTIONS

1. Preheat oven to 350°F. Coat a 9x5-inch loaf pan with butter or nonstick cooking spray and line the bottom with parchment paper.
2. In a medium bowl, whisk together flour, baking powder and salt.
3. In a large bowl, using an electric mixer, beat butter and sugar together on medium-high speed until light and fluffy, about 4 minutes. Scrape down the sides of the bowl with a rubber spatula. Add eggs, one at a time, and beat well after each addition. Add vanilla and beat just until combined. Add half the flour mixture and beat on low speed until combined. Scrape down the sides of the bowl with a rubber spatula. Add buttermilk and beat to combine. Add remaining flour mixture and beat just until combined.
4. To make the chocolate batter, in a medium bowl, mix cocoa powder and water until smooth. Add in ⅓ of the vanilla batter and stir until well combined.
5. Spoon ⅓ of the vanilla batter into bottom of prepared pan. Spoon ⅙ of remaining batter at a time on top of it to create a grid pattern of 6 squares (3 of each flavor), alternating between vanilla and chocolate (like a checkerboard). Use a butter knife to gently swirl batters together in a zigzag pattern, being careful not to overswirl.
6. Bake until toothpick inserted in center of cake comes out clean, 40 to 50 minutes. (Check cake after 30 minutes; if it's browning too quickly, tent with aluminum foil.) Cool in pan on wire rack for 15 minutes, then transfer cake directly to rack to cool completely.
NOTE You can make this cake a few days ahead of serving—it won't lose its moist texture and tender crumb. Store in an airtight container, or cover tightly with plastic wrap and keep at room temperature.

Ginger-Lemon Cake

Company-Worthy • Nut-Free

Fresh, ground and crystallized ginger come together for a zesty loaf cake you can enjoy any time of day.

PREP 20 minutes
BAKE 50 to 60 minutes
MAKES 1 loaf

INGREDIENTS

- 2 cups cake flour
- 2 teaspoons baking powder
- 1 tablespoon ground ginger
- ½ teaspoon kosher salt
- ¾ cup (1½ sticks) unsalted butter, at room temperature
- 1½ cups confectioners' sugar
- 1 tablespoon light corn syrup
- 4 large eggs
  Freshly grated zest of 1 lemon
  2-inch piece of fresh ginger, peeled and grated
- ½ teaspoon vanilla extract
- ¾ cup whole milk
- ½ cup crystallized ginger, chopped

INSTRUCTIONS

1. Preheat oven to 350°F. Coat a 9x5-inch loaf pan with butter or nonstick cooking spray and line the bottom with parchment paper.
2. In a medium bowl, whisk together flour, baking powder, ground ginger and salt.
3. In a large bowl, using an electric mixer, beat butter, sugar and corn syrup together on medium-high speed until light and fluffy, about 4 minutes. Scrape down the sides of the bowl with a rubber spatula. Add eggs, one at a time, and beat well after each addition. Add lemon zest, grated ginger and vanilla and beat just until combined. Scrape down the sides of the bowl. Using a rubber spatula, fold in half the flour mixture until combined. Fold in the milk, followed by the remaining flour mixture and crystallized ginger. Pour into prepared pan and smooth the top with an offset spatula or a butter knife.
4. Bake until toothpick inserted in center of cake comes out clean and top is golden brown, 50 to 60 minutes. (Check cake after 40 minutes; if it's browning too quickly, tent with aluminum foil.) Cool in pan on wire rack for 15 minutes, then transfer cake directly to rack to cool completely.

quick tip

A butter knife is all you'll need to make the beautiful swirl pattern in this chocolate and vanilla cake.

MARBLE POUND CAKE

Classic Pound Cake
Easy • Family Favorite
Make Ahead • Nut-Free

This versatile cake is delicious as is, but for an extra kick, drizzle any flavor of 5-Minute Icing (page 123) on top after baking.

PREP 15 minutes
BAKE 45 to 50 minutes
MAKES 1 loaf cake

INGREDIENTS
- 2 cups cake flour
- 2 teaspoons baking powder
- 1 teaspoon kosher salt
- ½ cup (1 stick) unsalted butter, at room temperature
- 1¼ cups sugar
- 3 large eggs
- 1 teaspoon vanilla extract
- ⅔ cup buttermilk
- 5-Minute Icing (optional)

INSTRUCTIONS
1. Preheat oven to 350°F. Coat a 9x5-inch loaf pan with butter or nonstick cooking spray and line the bottom with parchment paper.
2. In a medium bowl, whisk together flour, baking powder and salt.
3. In a large bowl, using an electric mixer, beat butter and sugar together on medium-high speed until light and fluffy, about 4 minutes. Scrape down the sides of the bowl with a rubber spatula. Add eggs, one at a time, and beat well after each addition. Add vanilla and beat just until combined. Add half the flour mixture and beat on low speed until combined. Scrape down the sides of the bowl. Add buttermilk and beat until combined. Add remaining flour mixture and beat just until combined. Pour into prepared pan and smooth the top with an offset spatula or butter knife.
4. Bake until toothpick inserted in center of cake comes out clean and top is golden brown, 40 to 50 minutes. (Check cake after 30 minutes; if it's browning too quickly, tent with aluminum foil.) Cool in pan on wire rack for 15 minutes, then transfer cake directly to rack to cool completely. Drizzle with icing, if using.
NOTE You can make this cake a few days ahead of serving—it won't lose its moist texture and tender crumb. Store in an airtight container or cover tightly with plastic wrap and keep at room temperature. Glaze the cake just before serving.

quick tip
Use this baking staple as the base layer in the Cranberry-Orange Trifle on page 115.

CINNAMON-
SUGAR
SWIRL BREAD

Cinnamon-Sugar Swirl Bread

Family Favorite • Make Ahead Nut-Free

This beautifully swirled quick bread is delicious on the day it's made. If you've got leftovers, slice and toast them and spread with butter.

PREP 25 minutes
BAKE 50 to 60 minutes
MAKES 1 loaf cake

INGREDIENTS

For the cinnamon sugar

- ⅓ cup granulated sugar
- ⅓ cup firmly packed light brown sugar
- 2 teaspoons ground cinnamon
- ¼ teaspoon ground nutmeg

For the cake

- 2 cups all-purpose flour
- 1 teaspoon baking powder
- ½ teaspoon baking soda
- 1 teaspoon kosher salt
- ½ cup (1 stick) unsalted butter, at room temperature
- 1 cup granulated sugar
- 2 large eggs
- 2 teaspoons vanilla extract
- 1 cup sour cream or plain, full-fat Greek yogurt

INSTRUCTIONS

1. Preheat oven to 350°F. Coat a 9x5-inch loaf pan with butter or nonstick cooking spray and dust lightly with flour.

2. To make the cinnamon sugar, in a medium bowl, stir together both sugars, cinnamon and nutmeg. Set aside.

3. To make the cake, in a medium bowl, whisk together flour, baking powder, baking soda and salt.

4. In a large bowl, using an electric mixer, beat butter and sugar together on medium-high speed until light and fluffy, about 3 minutes. Add eggs and vanilla and beat until combined. Add half the flour mixture and beat on low speed until combined. Add sour cream and beat until combined. Scrape down the sides of the bowl with a rubber spatula. Add remaining flour mixture and beat just until combined. (Batter will be thick.) Pour ⅓ of batter into prepared pan and smooth the top with an offset spatula or butter knife. Sprinkle half the cinnamon sugar evenly on top, using your fingers to gently press it down onto the batter. Top with another ⅓ of the batter and remaining cinnamon sugar, pressing gently to adhere. Top with remaining batter. Use a butter knife to swirl the cinnamon sugar into the batter in a zigzag pattern. Smooth the top.

5. Bake until toothpick inserted in center of bread comes out clean and top is golden brown, 50 to 60 minutes. (Check bread after 40 minutes; if it's browning too quickly, tent with aluminum foil.) Cool in pan on wire rack for 15 minutes, then transfer bread directly to rack to cool completely.

Date & Hazelnut Quick Bread

Company-Worthy • Easy • Gift Idea

You can swap the hazelnuts for any nut you have on hand—pecans or walnuts especially would be right at home here.

PREP 15 minutes
BAKE 50 to 60 minutes
MAKES 1 loaf

INGREDIENTS

- 2 cups all-purpose flour
- 2 teaspoons baking powder
- ½ teaspoon ground cinnamon
- 1 teaspoon kosher salt
- 1 cup (2 sticks) unsalted butter, at room temperature
- ½ cup (4 ounces) cream cheese, at room temperature
- ¾ cup firmly packed light brown sugar
- 4 large eggs
- 1 teaspoon vanilla extract
- 1 cup dates, pitted and chopped
- 1 cup hazelnuts, chopped

INSTRUCTIONS

1. Preheat oven to 350°F. Coat a 9x5-inch loaf pan with butter or nonstick cooking spray and line the bottom with parchment paper.

2. In a medium bowl, whisk together flour, baking powder, cinnamon and salt.

3. In a large bowl, using an electric mixer, beat butter, cream cheese and sugar together on medium-high speed until light and fluffy, about 4 minutes. Scrape down the sides of the bowl with a rubber spatula. Add eggs, one at a time, and beat well after each addition. Add vanilla and beat just until combined. Scrape down the sides of the bowl. Add flour mixture and beat on low speed until combined. Using a rubber spatula, fold in dates and hazelnuts. Pour into prepared pan and smooth the top with an offset spatula or a butter knife.

4. Bake until toothpick inserted in center of bread comes out clean and top is golden brown, approximately 50 to 60 minutes. (Check bread after 40 minutes; if it's browning too quickly, tent with aluminum foil.) Cool in pan on wire rack for 20 minutes, then transfer bread directly to rack to cool completely.

CHRISTMAS TREE
CUPCAKES, PAGE 100

Chapter 7

Cupcakes

FUN AND FESTIVE DECORATING
IDEAS TRANSFORM THESE SWEET
TREATS INTO WINTER WONDERS.

Mini Citrus Tea Cakes
Easy • Nut-Free

You can use fresh lemons or oranges to flavor these tiny treats, which are finished with a drizzle of tangy icing and sprinkled with poppy seeds. It's easiest to zest citrus before you juice it.

PREP 10 minutes
BAKE 16 to 18 minutes
MAKES 3 dozen mini cupcakes

INGREDIENTS

- 1½ cups all-purpose flour
- 2 teaspoons baking powder
- 1 teaspoon kosher salt
- 1 cup sugar
- 2 large eggs
- 1 to 2 teaspoons freshly grated lemon or orange zest
- ¼ cup freshly squeezed lemon or orange juice
- ½ cup sour cream or plain, full-fat Greek Yogurt
- ½ cup (1 stick) unsalted butter, melted
  5-Minute Lemon or 5-Minute Orange Icing (page 123)
  Poppy seeds, for decorating (optional)

INSTRUCTIONS

1. Preheat oven to 350°F. Line 2 mini muffin pans with paper or foil liners.
2. In a large bowl, whisk together flour, baking powder and salt.
3. In a medium bowl, whisk together sugar, eggs, lemon (or orange) zest and juice, and sour cream. Add wet mixture to flour mixture and stir just until combined. Using a rubber spatula, fold in melted butter. Divide evenly among prepared muffin cups, each no more than ⅔ full.
4. Bake until a toothpick inserted into the center of cupcake comes out clean and tops are light golden brown, 16 to 18 minutes. Cool on wire rack for 10 minutes, then transfer cupcakes directly to rack to cool completely.
5. While cupcakes are cooling, make the icing. Spoon icing over each cupcake and sprinkle with poppy seeds, if using.

quick tip

As their name implies, these tangy and subtly sweet cakes are perfect with a cup of tea (or coffee) any time of day.

Chocolate-Peppermint Cupcakes

Easy • Family Favorite
Nut-Free

No holiday season is complete without this festive flavor combination.

PREP 20 minutes
BAKE 18 to 20 minutes
MAKES 2 dozen cupcakes

INGREDIENTS

- 2 cups all-purpose flour
- ½ cup unsweetened cocoa powder
- 1½ teaspoons baking soda
- 1 teaspoon kosher salt
- ¾ cup (1½ sticks) unsalted butter, at room temperature
- 1 cup granulated sugar
- 1 cup firmly packed light brown sugar
- 2 large eggs
- 1 teaspoon vanilla extract
- 1 teaspoon peppermint extract
- 1 cup buttermilk
- ½ cup sour cream
  Chocolate Frosting (page 121)
  Candy canes or peppermint candies, for decorating (optional)

INSTRUCTIONS

1. Preheat oven to 350°F. Line two 12-cup muffin pans with paper or foil liners.

2. In a medium bowl, whisk together flour, cocoa powder, baking soda and salt.

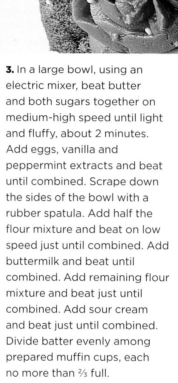

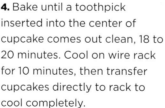

3. In a large bowl, using an electric mixer, beat butter and both sugars together on medium-high speed until light and fluffy, about 2 minutes. Add eggs, vanilla and peppermint extracts and beat until combined. Scrape down the sides of the bowl with a rubber spatula. Add half the flour mixture and beat on low speed just until combined. Add buttermilk and beat until combined. Add remaining flour mixture and beat just until combined. Add sour cream and beat just until combined. Divide batter evenly among prepared muffin cups, each no more than ⅔ full.

4. Bake until a toothpick inserted into the center of cupcake comes out clean, 18 to 20 minutes. Cool on wire rack for 10 minutes, then transfer cupcakes directly to rack to cool completely.

5. While the cupcakes cool, make the frosting. Place candy canes or peppermint candies in a sealed zip-close bag and crush them with a rolling pin or meat pounder, leaving a few bigger chunks.

6. Using a pastry bag fitted with a star tip (we used Ateco 852), or an offset spatula or butter knife, top the cupcakes with frosting and decorate with crushed candy.

1   teaspoon green gel food
     coloring, plus more as needed
     Rainbow sprinkles or
     nonpareils, for decorating
     Iced, small, star-shaped
     sugar cookies (page 35,
     optional)

INSTRUCTIONS

1. Preheat oven to 350°F.
Line two 12-cup muffin pans
with paper or foil liners.
2. In a medium bowl, whisk together
flour, baking powder and salt.
3. In a large bowl, using an electric
mixer, beat butter and sugar
together on medium-high speed
until light and fluffy, about
2 minutes. Add eggs, one at a time,
beating well after each addition.
Add vanilla and beat until
combined. Scrape down the sides
of the bowl with a rubber spatula.
Add half the flour mixture and beat
on low speed just until combined.
Add milk, then remaining flour
mixture and beat just until
combined. Divide batter evenly
among prepared muffin cups, each
no more than ⅔ full.
4. Bake until a toothpick inserted
into the center of cupcake comes
out clean and tops are light golden
brown, 18 to 20 minutes, rotating
pans halfway for even baking. Cool
on wire rack for 10 minutes, then
transfer cupcakes directly to rack
to cool completely.
5. While the cupcakes cool,
make the frosting. Add the green
food coloring and mix well until
combined, adding more, if needed,
until desired color is achieved.
6. Fit a pastry bag with a star tip
(we used Ateco 852). Pipe frosting
onto cupcakes, starting with
a wide base and gradually getting
narrower toward the top to
resemble a tree. Top with sprinkles
to resemble ornaments and add a
star cookie, if using.

Christmas Tree Cupcakes

Easy • Family Favorite • Nut-Free

*Pipe a tall layer of green frosting
onto classic vanilla cupcakes
and decorate them as simply or
elaborately as you like.*

PREP   20 minutes
BAKE   18 to 20 minutes
MAKES 2 dozen cupcakes

INGREDIENTS

2½ cups all-purpose flour
2½ teaspoons baking
     powder
1   teaspoon kosher salt
¾   cup (1½ sticks) unsalted
     butter, at room temperature
1½ cups sugar
4   large eggs
2   teaspoons vanilla extract
⅔   cup whole milk
     Vanilla Frosting (page 122)

Cranberry Cupcakes With Orange Icing
Easy • Gift Idea • Nut-Free

A popular muffin gets its star turn as a cupcake! If you don't have orange extract on hand for the icing, replace the milk with orange juice instead.

PREP 15 minutes
BAKE 20 to 25 minutes
MAKES 2 dozen cupcakes

INGREDIENTS

- 2½ cups all-purpose flour
- 1 teaspoon baking powder
- ½ teaspoon baking soda
- 1½ teaspoons ground cinnamon
- ½ teaspoon ground nutmeg
  Pinch of ground cloves
- ½ teaspoon kosher salt
- 2 cups sugar
- 4 large eggs
- 1 cup canola or vegetable oil
- 2 teaspoons vanilla extract
- 1 teaspoon freshly grated orange zest
- 1 cup sour cream
- 1½ cups fresh or thawed, frozen cranberries, chopped
  5-Minute Orange Icing (page 123)
  Colored sugar, for decorating

INSTRUCTIONS

1. Preheat oven to 350°F. Line two 12-cup muffin pans with paper or foil liners.
2. In a medium bowl, whisk together flour, baking powder, baking soda,` cinnamon, nutmeg, cloves and salt.
3. In a large bowl, using an electric mixer, beat sugar and eggs together on medium-high speed until pale and thick, 2 minutes. Add oil, vanilla and orange zest and beat until combined. Add half the flour mixture and beat on low speed until combined. Add sour cream, then remaining flour mixture; beat until combined. Using a rubber spatula, fold in cranberries. Divide batter evenly among prepared muffin cups, each no more than ⅔ full.
4. Bake until a toothpick inserted into the center of cupcake comes out clean and tops are light golden brown, 20 to 25 minutes. Cool on wire rack for 10 minutes, then transfer cupcakes directly to rack to cool completely.
5. While the cupcakes cool, make the icing. Spoon over cupcakes; sprinkle with colored sugar.

Mini Banana-Chocolate Cupcakes

Easy • Family Favorite
Nut-Free

Little hands won't be able to get enough of these one-bite banana treats.

PREP 15 minutes
BAKE 14 to 16 minutes
MAKES 4 dozen mini cupcakes

INGREDIENTS

- 1½ cups all-purpose flour
- 1 teaspoon baking soda
- 1 teaspoon salt
- ½ cup (1 stick) unsalted butter, at room temperature
- 1 cup sugar
- 2 large eggs
- 1 cup mashed bananas (about 2 large, very ripe)
- ¾ cup sour cream
- 2 teaspoons vanilla extract
- 1 cup mini semisweet chocolate chips
  Chocolate Frosting (page 121)

INSTRUCTIONS

1. Preheat oven to 350°F. Line 2 mini muffin pans with paper or foil liners.

2. In a medium bowl, whisk together flour, baking soda and salt.

3. In a large bowl, using an electric mixer, beat butter and sugar together on medium-high speed until light and fluffy, about 2 minutes. Add eggs and beat until combined. Scrape down the bowl with a rubber spatula. Add flour mixture and beat on low speed just until combined. Add bananas, sour cream and vanilla and beat until combined. Using a rubber spatula, fold in chocolate chips. Divide batter evenly among prepared muffin cups, each no more than ⅔ full.

4. Bake until a toothpick inserted into the center of cupcake comes out clean and tops are light golden brown, 14 to 16 minutes. Cool on wire rack for 10 minutes, then transfer cupcakes directly to rack to cool completely.

5. While the cupcakes cool, make the frosting. Using a pastry bag fitted with a star tip (we used Ateco 852), or an offset spatula or butter knife, top the cupcakes with frosting. (You might not need to use all of the frosting.)

quick tip

If you don't have two mini muffin pans, refrigerate the remaining batter until the first batch of cupcakes has finished baking.

Black Forest Cupcakes
Family Favorite • Nut-Free

A cherry-filled center is a sweet surprise inside a classic holiday flavor combo of chocolate and whipped cream.

PREP 20 minutes
BAKE 18 to 20 minutes
MAKES 2 dozen cupcakes

INGREDIENTS

- 2 cups all-purpose flour
- ½ cup unsweetened cocoa powder, plus more for dusting
- 1½ teaspoons baking soda
- 1 teaspoon kosher salt
- ¾ cup (1½ sticks) unsalted butter, at room temperature
- 1 cup granulated sugar
- 1 cup firmly packed light brown sugar
- 2 large eggs
- 1 teaspoon vanilla extract
- 1 cup buttermilk
- ½ cup sour cream
- 1 cup cherry jam or preserves
  Whipped Cream Frosting (page 122)
  Chocolate flakes and red sprinkles, for decorating

INSTRUCTIONS

1. Preheat oven to 350°F. Line two 12-cup muffin pans with paper or foil liners.

2. In a medium bowl, whisk together flour, cocoa powder, baking soda and salt.

3. In a large bowl, using an electric mixer, beat butter and both sugars together on medium-high speed until light and fluffy, about 2 minutes. Add eggs and vanilla and beat until combined. Scrape down the sides of the bowl with a rubber spatula. Add half the flour mixture and beat on low speed just until combined. Add buttermilk and beat until combined. Add remaining flour mixture and beat just until incorporated. Add sour cream and beat just until combined. Divide batter evenly among prepared muffin cups, each no more than ⅔ full.

4. Bake until a toothpick inserted into the center of cupcake comes out clean, 18 to 20 minutes. Cool on wire rack for 10 minutes, then transfer cupcakes directly to rack to cool completely.

5. While the cupcakes cool, make the frosting.

6. Using a small, sharp knife, cut a 1½-inch round about 1 inch deep in the center of each cupcake, then remove the rounds. Cut each round in half crosswise. Fill each hole with a spoonful of cherry jam. Cover hole with top half of round.

7. Using a pastry bag that's fitted with a drop flower tip (we used Wilton 2D), or an offset spatula or butter knife, top the cupcakes with frosting and decorate with flakes and sprinkles.

White Chocolate-Raspberry Cupcakes

Family Favorite • Nut-Free

Raspberries play double duty in this luscious cupcake—freeze-dried raspberries flavor the cake, while raspberry jam perks up the frosting.

PREP 15 minutes
BAKE 18 to 20 minutes
MAKES 2 dozen cupcakes

INGREDIENTS

- 2 cups all-purpose flour
- 1 cup freeze-dried raspberries, crushed
- 2½ teaspoons baking powder
- 1 teaspoon kosher salt
- ¾ cup (1½ sticks) unsalted butter, at room temperature
- 1½ cups sugar
- 4 large eggs
- 1 teaspoon vanilla extract
- ⅔ cup whole milk
- 1 cup white chocolate chips
  Cream Cheese Frosting (page 121)
- ½ cup raspberry jam
  White chocolate shavings, for decorating

INSTRUCTIONS

1. Preheat oven to 350°F. Line two 12-cup muffin pans with paper or foil liners.

2. In a medium bowl, whisk together flour, freeze-dried raspberries, baking powder and salt.

3. In a large bowl, using an electric mixer, beat butter and sugar together on medium-high speed until light and fluffy, about 2 minutes. Add eggs, one at a time, beating well after each addition. Add vanilla and beat until combined. Add half the flour mixture and beat on low speed just until combined. Add milk, then remaining flour mixture and beat just until combined. Using a rubber spatula, fold in chocolate chips. Divide batter evenly among prepared muffin cups, each no more than ⅔ full.

4. Bake until a toothpick inserted into the center of cupcake comes out clean and tops are light golden brown, 18 to 20 minutes. Cool on wire rack for 10 minutes, then transfer cupcakes directly to rack to cool completely.

5. While the cupcakes cool, make the frosting. Fold in raspberry jam just until combined.

6. Using a pastry bag fitted with a star tip (we used Wilton 8B), or an offset spatula or butter knife, top the cupcakes with frosting, then sprinkle with white chocolate shavings.

quick tip

Look for gold, silver, red or green foil muffin liners to add a festive touch to your cupcakes.

quick tip
A cupcake plunger or corer makes easy work of removing the centers so you can fill them with marshmallow cream.

HOT COCOA CUPCAKES

Hot Cocoa Cupcakes

Family Favorite • Nut-Free

Reinvent your favorite cozy winter drink as a cupcake filled with marshmallow cream and topped with whipped cream frosting.

PREP 20 minutes

BAKE 18 to 20 minutes

MAKES 2 dozen cupcakes

INGREDIENTS

- 2 cups all-purpose flour
- ½ cup unsweetened cocoa powder, plus more for dusting
- 1½ teaspoons baking soda
- 1 teaspoon kosher salt
- ¾ cup (1½ sticks) unsalted butter, at room temperature
- 1 cup granulated sugar
- 1 cup firmly packed light brown sugar
- 2 large eggs
- 1 teaspoon vanilla extract
- 1 cup buttermilk
- ½ cup sour cream
- 1 cup marshmallow cream Whipped Cream Frosting (page 122)

INSTRUCTIONS

1. Preheat oven to 350°F. Line two 12-cup muffin pans with paper or foil liners.

2. In a medium bowl, whisk together flour, cocoa powder, baking soda and salt.

3. In a large bowl, using an electric mixer, beat butter and both sugars together on medium-high speed until light and fluffy, about 2 minutes. Add eggs and vanilla and beat until combined. Scrape down the sides of the bowl with a rubber spatula. Add half the flour mixture and beat on low speed just until combined. Add buttermilk and beat until combined. Add remaining flour mixture and beat just until combined. Add sour cream and beat just until combined. Divide batter evenly among prepared muffin cups, each no more than ⅔ full.

4. Bake until a toothpick inserted into the center of cupcake comes out clean, 18 to 20 minutes. Cool on wire rack for 10 minutes, then transfer cupcakes directly to rack to cool completely.

5. While the cupcakes cool, make the frosting.

6. Using a small, sharp knife, cut a 1½-inch round about 1 inch deep in the center of each cupcake, then remove the rounds. Cut each round in half crosswise. Fill each hole with a spoonful of marshmallow cream. Cover hole with top half of round.

7. Using a pastry bag fitted with a star tip (we used Wilton 8B), or an offset spatula or butter knife, top the cupcakes with frosting and dust with cocoa powder.

Pumpkin-Spice Cupcakes With Brown Sugar-Cream Cheese Frosting

Easy • Family Favorite • Nut-Free

Get all the flavors of pumpkin pie in individual servings with these quick and easy cupcakes—perfect throughout the holiday season.

PREP 15 minutes

BAKE 20 to 22 minutes

MAKES 2 dozen cupcakes

INGREDIENTS

- 3 cups all-purpose flour
- 2 cups sugar
- 2 teaspoons baking soda
- 2 teaspoons ground cinnamon
- 1½ teaspoons ground allspice
- 1½ teaspoons kosher salt
- ½ cup canola or vegetable oil
- 4 large eggs
- ½ cup cold water
- 2 cups canned or cooked pumpkin (do not use pumpkin pie filling) Brown Sugar-Cream Cheese Frosting (page 121)

INSTRUCTIONS

1. Preheat oven to 350°F. Line two 12-cup muffin pans with paper or foil liners.

2. In a large bowl, whisk together flour, sugar, baking soda, cinnamon, allspice and salt.

3. In another large bowl, whisk together oil, eggs, water and pumpkin. Add flour mixture to wet ingredients and mix with a wooden spoon just until combined. Divide evenly among prepared muffin cups, each no more than ⅔ full.

4. Bake cupcakes until a toothpick inserted into center of one comes out clean, about 20 to 22 minutes. Cool in pan on wire rack for 10 minutes, then transfer the cupcakes directly to a wire rack to cool completely.

5. While the cupcakes cool, make the frosting.

6. Using a pastry bag fitted with a star tip (we used Wilton 8B), or an offset spatula or a butter knife, top the cupcakes with the frosting.

Coconut Cupcakes
Classic • Family Favorite • Nut-Free

You can't miss the coco-nutty flavor in these luscious treats. A teaspoon of coconut extract takes the cream cheese frosting to the next level (but you can leave it out if you don't have any on hand). Toasting extra shredded coconut allows for a pretty, and delicious, topping.

PREP 25 minutes
BAKE 18 to 20 minutes
MAKES 2 dozen cupcakes

INGREDIENTS

- 1½ **cups sweetened, shredded coconut**
- 1 **cup coconut milk**
- 3 **large eggs**
- 1 **teaspoon vanilla extract**
- 2¼ **cups all-purpose flour, plus more for dusting**
- 1½ **cups sugar**
- 3 **teaspoons baking powder**
- 1 **teaspoon kosher salt**
- 1 **cup (2 sticks) unsalted butter, at room temperature, cut into cubes**
  Cream Cheese Frosting (page 121)
- 1 **teaspoon coconut extract (optional)**

INSTRUCTIONS

1. Preheat oven to 325°F. Line two 12-cup muffin pans with paper or foil liners.
2. Line a baking sheet with parchment paper. Spread shredded coconut evenly across the prepared baking sheet and toast until light brown, 3 to 4 minutes. Cool on wire rack while you make the cake. Set aside ½ cup for decorating.
3. In a large measuring cup or medium bowl, whisk together coconut milk, eggs and vanilla.
4. In a large bowl, whisk together flour, sugar, baking powder and salt. Using a rubber spatula, fold in the toasted coconut. Using an electric mixer, beat in butter on low speed until crumbly, about 1 minute. Add coconut milk mixture and beat until combined, 1 minute. Divide batter evenly among prepared muffin cups, each no more than ⅔ full.
5. Bake until a toothpick inserted into the center of cupcake comes out clean and tops are light golden brown, 18 to 20 minutes. Cool on wire rack for 10 minutes, then transfer cupcakes directly to rack to cool completely.
6. While the cupcakes cool, make the frosting. Add the coconut extract, if using.
7. Using a pastry bag fitted with a round tip (we used Wilton 8B), or an offset spatula or butter knife, top the cupcakes with frosting and decorate with the reserved toasted coconut.

Snowmen Cupcakes

Easy • Family Favorite • Nut-Free

A few marshmallows and sprinkles are all you'll need to create these adorable, edible snowmen.

PREP 20 minutes
BAKE 18 to 20 minutes
MAKES 2 dozen cupcakes

INGREDIENTS

- 2 cups all-purpose flour
- ½ cup unsweetened cocoa powder, plus more for dusting
- 1½ teaspoons baking soda
- 1 teaspoon kosher salt
- ¾ cup (1½ sticks) unsalted butter, at room temperature
- 1 cup granulated sugar
- 1 cup firmly packed light brown sugar
- 2 large eggs
- 1 teaspoon vanilla extract
- 1 cup buttermilk
- ½ cup sour cream
  Vanilla Frosting (page 122) or Cream Cheese Frosting (page 121)

For decorating

- 48 jumbo marshmallows
- Black and orange sprinkles
- White sanding sugar

INSTRUCTIONS

1. Preheat oven to 350°F. Line two 12-cup muffin pans with paper or foil liners.

2. In a medium bowl, whisk together flour, cocoa powder, baking soda and salt.

3. In a large bowl, using an electric mixer, beat butter and both sugars together on medium-high speed until light and fluffy, about 2 minutes. Add eggs and vanilla and beat until combined. Scrape down the sides of the bowl with a rubber spatula. Add half the flour mixture and beat on low speed just until combined. Add buttermilk and beat until combined. Add remaining flour mixture and beat just until combined. Add sour cream and

beat just until combined. Divide batter evenly among prepared muffin cups, each no more than ⅔ full.

4. Bake until a toothpick inserted into the center of cupcake comes out clean, 18 to 20 minutes. Cool on wire rack for 10 minutes, then transfer cupcakes directly to rack to cool completely.

5. While the cupcakes cool, make the frosting.

6. To assemble the snowmen, using a small, sharp knife, cut a thin layer off the top of 24 marshmallows. Press the sticky, cut side to an uncut marshmallow for each snowman. Stick 2 chocolate sprinkles into the top marshmallow for eyes and

1 orange sprinkle for a nose. Stick 3 chocolate sprinkles in a vertical line into the bottom marshmallow for buttons.

7. Using a pastry bag fitted with a round tip (we used Wilton 10), or an offset spatula or butter knife, top the cupcakes with frosting. Sprinkle with sanding sugar, then place one marshmallow snowman in the center of each cupcake.

quick tip

Halloween-themed black and orange sprinkles are perfect for decorating these snowmen cupcakes, so save a few after scary season ends.

quick tip

Filling a pastry bag with two colors of icing—one on each side—creates this pretty swirl effect.

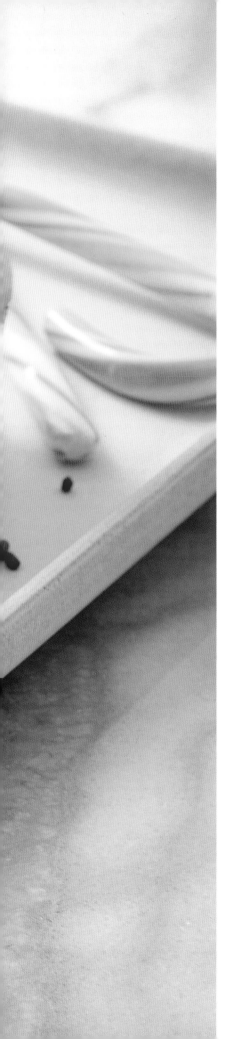

Vanilla Swirl Cupcakes
Company-Worthy • Easy • Nut-Free

A teaspoon of peppermint extract added to the frosting will make these festive cupcakes taste like candy canes.

PREP 20 minutes
BAKE 18 to 20 minutes
MAKES 2 dozen cupcakes

INGREDIENTS
- 2½ cups all-purpose flour
- 2½ teaspoons baking powder
- 1 teaspoon kosher salt
- ¾ cup (1½ sticks) unsalted butter, at room temperature
- 1½ cups sugar
- 4 large eggs
- 2 teaspoons vanilla extract
- ⅔ cup whole milk
  Vanilla or Peppermint Frosting (both, page 122)
- 1 teaspoon red gel food coloring, plus more as desired
  Red and/or white sanding sugar or sprinkles, for decorating (optional)

INSTRUCTIONS
1. Preheat oven to 350°F. Line two 12-cup muffin pans with paper or foil liners.

2. In a medium bowl, whisk together flour, baking powder and salt.

3. In a large bowl, using an electric mixer, beat butter and sugar together on medium-high speed until light and fluffy, about 2 minutes. Add eggs, one at a time, beating well after each addition. Add vanilla and beat until combined. Scrape down sides of the bowl with a rubber spatula. Add half the flour mixture and beat on low speed just until combined. Add milk, then remaining flour mixture and beat just until combined. Divide batter evenly among prepared muffin cups, each no more than ⅔ full.

4. Bake until a toothpick inserted into the center of cupcake comes out clean and tops are light golden brown, 18 to 20 minutes, rotating pans halfway for even baking. Cool on wire rack for 10 minutes, then transfer cupcakes directly to rack to cool completely.

5. While the cupcakes cool, make the frosting. Place ½ the frosting in a medium bowl. Add red food coloring and mix well until combined, adding more, if needed, until desired color is achieved.

6. Fit a pastry bag with a star tip (we used Wilton 2D). Transfer red frosting to the pastry bag, keeping it on one side; transfer white frosting to the other side of the pastry bag (this will create a swirl effect). Pipe frosting onto cupcakes and decorate with sanding sugar or sprinkles as desired.

PUMPKIN
CHEESECAKE,
PAGE 115

Chapter 8

Specialty Cakes, Icings, Frostings and Fillings

CHEESECAKE, UPSIDE-DOWN CREATIONS,
TRIFLE AND GINGERBREAD MINI CONFECTIONS
ARE ALL FESTIVE WAYS TO IMPRESS YOUR GUESTS.
PLUS: ESSENTIAL AND FUN FINISHING TOUCHES.

CRANBERRY-ORANGE
TRIFLE

Cranberry-Orange Trifle

Company-Worthy • Make Ahead
Nut-Free

This variation on a classic English dessert uses seasonal ingredients for a spectacular end to a holiday meal.

PREP 30 minutes
CHILL 2 hours or up to overnight
MAKES 12 servings

INGREDIENTS

Classic Pound Cake (page 91) or use store-bought

For the compote
- 2 cups fresh or frozen cranberries
- 1 cup granulated sugar
- ¼ cup orange juice
- 1 tablespoon freshly grated orange zest
- 2 teaspoons peeled and grated fresh ginger

For the filling
- 1 (8-ounce) package cream cheese, at room temperature
- ½ cup firmly packed light brown sugar
- ½ teaspoon vanilla extract
- 1½ cups heavy cream

INSTRUCTIONS

1. Bake and cool pound cake as directed.
2. To make the compote, in a medium saucepan set on the stovetop over medium heat, combine cranberries, granulated sugar, orange juice, orange zest and ginger. Bring to a simmer and cook until cranberries begin to burst, 8 to 10 minutes. Set aside to cool.
3. To make the filling, in a large bowl, using an electric mixer, beat cream cheese, brown sugar and vanilla together on medium-high speed until combined. Add heavy cream and beat on medium speed until smooth.
4. To assemble the trifle, cut pound cake into ¾-inch-thick slices. Arrange ⅓ of slices in a layer in the bottom of a large serving dish (preferably glass, so you can see the layers), cutting slices as needed so they fit snugly. Top with ⅓ of compote and then ⅓ of filling, spreading each layer evenly to the sides of the dish. Repeat layers twice more. Cover tightly with plastic wrap and refrigerate until set, at least 2 hours or up to overnight. Slice into wedges or spoon out servings.

Pumpkin Cheesecake

Family Favorite • Make Ahead
Nut-Free

Top this delicious treat with a dollop of whipped cream or crème fraîche.

PREP 25 minutes
CHILL overnight
BAKE 1 hour 10 minutes to 1 hour 25 minutes, in 2 parts
MAKES 10 to 12 servings

INGREDIENTS

For the crust
- 10 ounces gingersnap cookies
- ¼ teaspoon kosher salt
- ½ cup (1 stick) butter, melted

For the filling
- 2 (8-ounce) packages cream cheese, at room temperature
- 1 cup firmly packed light brown sugar
- 5 large eggs
- 2 cups canned or cooked pumpkin (don't use pumpkin pie filling)
- ½ teaspoon ground allspice
- ¼ teaspoon ground ginger
- 1½ teaspoons ground cinnamon, plus more for sprinkling
- 1 teaspoon vanilla extract
  Pinch of kosher salt
  Whipped cream or crème fraîche, for serving (optional)

INSTRUCTIONS

1. Preheat oven to 350°F. Coat the sides of a 9-inch round springform pan with nonstick cooking spray or butter. Cover the bottom of the pan and halfway up the outside with aluminum foil (this will help keep water from seeping inside while baking).
2. To make the crust, in a food processor, combine cookies and salt and pulse until crumbs form. Add melted butter and pulse until crumbs resemble rough sand. Press evenly into prepared pan.
3. Bake until just lightly toasted, 8 to 10 minutes. Cool on wire rack.
4. To make the filling, in a large bowl, using an electric mixer (or a stand mixer fitted with paddle attachment), beat cream cheese and sugar together on medium speed until well combined, about 3 minutes. Add eggs, one at a time, and beat until combined. Add pumpkin, allspice, ginger, cinnamon, vanilla and salt and beat until combined. Pour batter over crust.
5. Place springform pan in a large roasting pan. Pull out oven rack and place roasting pan on rack. Pour boiling water into roasting pan, coming two-thirds of the way up the side of the springform pan. Bake until firm, 60 to 75 minutes. Cool completely on wire rack. Cover with plastic wrap and refrigerate overnight. To serve, sprinkle with cinnamon and top with whipped cream, if desired.

quick tip

If you have a few sizes of gingerbread people cutters, you can shape and decorate an entire family!

Gingerbread People Mini Cakes

Easy • Family Favorite • Nut-Free

These cakes are a fun alternative to cookies. Metal cutters work best; they keep the edges smoother.

PREP 15 minutes
BAKE 20 to 25 minutes
MAKES about 8 mini cakes

INGREDIENTS

- 1½ cups all-purpose flour
- 1 tablespoon ground ginger
- 2 teaspoons ground cinnamon
- ½ teaspoon ground nutmeg
- ¼ teaspoon ground cloves
- 1 teaspoon kosher salt
- 1½ cups (3 sticks) unsalted butter, at room temperature
- 1½ cups sugar
- ¼ cup unsulfured molasses
- 1 teaspoon vanilla extract
- 4 large eggs
  5-Minute Icing (page 123)
  Small candies for decorating

INSTRUCTIONS

1. Preheat oven to 350°F. Coat a 13x9-inch baking pan with nonstick cooking spray or butter and line with parchment paper, letting it hang slightly over the edges. Spray or butter the parchment.

2. In a medium bowl, whisk together flour, ginger, cinnamon, nutmeg, cloves and salt.

3. In a large bowl, using an electric mixer, beat butter and sugar together on medium-high speed until light and fluffy, about 2 minutes. Add molasses and vanilla and beat until combined. Add eggs, one at a time, and beat until combined. Scrape down the sides of the bowl with a rubber spatula. Add flour mixture and beat on low speed just until combined. Pour into prepared pan.

4. Bake until toothpick inserted into center of cake comes out clean and top is golden brown, 20 to 25 minutes. Cool completely in pan on wire rack.

5. Using parchment paper as handles, remove cake from pan. Using a gingerbread person cookie cutter, cut out shapes from the cake, spacing them as close together as possible. (Enjoy the scraps as a baker's treat!) Fit a pastry bag with a small round tip and fill with icing. Pipe dots for eyes, nose, buttons and other decorations, as desired. While icing is wet, press tiny candies into it, as desired.

Cranberry Upside-Down Cake

Family Favorite • Nut-Free

Use lemon zest for more tang or orange zest for a stronger citrus flavor in the cranberry topping.

PREP 20 minutes
BAKE 45 minutes
MAKES 8 to 10 servings

INGREDIENTS

- ¼ cup (½ stick) unsalted butter
- 3/4 cup firmly packed light brown sugar
- 2 cups fresh or thawed frozen cranberries
- 1¼ cups all-purpose flour
- ½ teaspoon baking powder
- ¼ teaspoon baking soda
- ½ teaspoon ground cinnamon
- 1 teaspoon kosher salt
- 1 large egg
- 1 cup granulated sugar
- ½ cup canola or vegetable oil
- 1 teaspoon vanilla extract
  Freshly grated zest of 1 lemon or 1 orange
- ½ cup sour cream
  Confectioners' sugar, for serving (optional)

INSTRUCTIONS

1. Preheat oven to 350°F. Coat a 9-inch round cake pan with nonstick cooking spray or butter. Line the bottom with parchment paper and spray or butter the paper.

2. In a small saucepan set on the stovetop over medium-low heat, combine butter and brown sugar. Cook until melted, stirring occasionally. Pour glaze into the prepared pan, swirling the pan to coat evenly. Arrange cranberries over glaze.

3. In a medium bowl, whisk together flour, baking powder, baking soda, cinnamon and salt.

4. In a large bowl, using an electric mixer, beat egg and granulated sugar together on medium speed until light and fluffy, about 2 minutes. Add oil, vanilla and lemon or orange zest and beat on low speed until combined. Add sour cream and beat just until combined. Add flour mixture and beat just until combined. Pour over cranberries and spread evenly with a rubber or offset spatula.

5. Bake until toothpick inserted into center of cake comes out clean, about 45 minutes. Cool in pan on wire rack for 10 minutes.

6. Loosen edges of cake with a butter knife or offset spatula. Cover the pan with a large plate, flip over and invert cake onto the plate. Carefully lift off the pan; remove and discard the parchment. Dust with confectioners' sugar, if desired.

117

Gingersnap Cheesecake With Sugared Cranberries
Make Ahead • Nut-Free

Bake cheesecake in a water bath to keep the texture moist and light and prevent cracking. Wrapping the bottom of the pan in aluminum foil keeps water from seeping in.

PREP 25 minutes

CHILL overnight

BAKE 1 hour 25 minutes to 1 hour 40 minutes, in 2 parts

MAKES 10 to 12 servings

INGREDIENTS
For the crust
- 10 ounces gingersnap cookies
- ¼ teaspoon kosher salt
- ½ cup (1 stick) butter, melted

For the filling
- 4 (8-ounce) packages of cream cheese, at room temperature
- ½ cup heavy cream
- 1½ cups sugar
- 4 large eggs
- 2 teaspoons freshly grated lemon zest
- ¼ cup fresh lemon juice
- 1 teaspoon vanilla extract
- ¼ teaspoon kosher salt

For the sugared cranberries
- ½ cup granulated sugar
- ½ cup water
- 1 cup cranberries, picked over and rinsed
- ¼ cup superfine sugar

INSTRUCTIONS
1. Preheat oven to 325°F. Coat sides of a 9-inch round springform pan with nonstick cooking spray or butter. Cover bottom of pan and halfway up the outside with aluminum foil (this will keep water from seeping inside while baking).

2. To make the crust, in a food processor, combine cookies and salt and pulse until crumbs form. Add melted butter and pulse until crumbs resemble rough sand. Press evenly into prepared pan.

3. Bake until just lightly toasted, about 8 to 10 minutes. Cool on wire rack.

4. To make the filling, in a large bowl, using an electric mixer (or a stand mixer fitted with paddle attachment), beat cream cheese, heavy cream and sugar together on medium speed until well combined, about 2 minutes. Add eggs, one at a time, and beat until combined. Add lemon zest, lemon juice, vanilla and salt and beat until combined. Pour batter over the crust.

5. Place springform pan in a large roasting pan. Pull out oven rack and place roasting pan on rack. Pour boiling water into roasting pan, coming two-thirds of the way up the side of the springform pan. Bake until firm, 75 to 90 minutes. (Check cheesecake after 1 hour. If it's starting to brown, cover top with aluminum foil.) Turn off oven and let cool completely in oven with oven door ajar. Cover with plastic wrap and refrigerate overnight.

6. To make the sugared cranberries, in a medium saucepan set on the stovetop over medium heat, whisk water and granulated sugar to combine. Bring to a simmer and whisk until sugar is dissolved. Remove from heat and stir in the cranberries to coat evenly. Cover and let steep for 10 minutes. Strain cranberries (you can reserve the cranberry simple syrup for drinks) and spread out onto a sheet of parchment paper set over a wire cooling rack. Dry for one hour. Roll cranberries in superfine sugar to coat.

7. Carefully remove cheesecake from springform pan. Decorate with sugared cranberries on top.

quick tip

To make your own superfine sugar, pulse granulated sugar in a food processor a few times until desired consistency is achieved.

CREAM CHEESE
FROSTING

Chocolate Frosting
Easy • Family Favorite • Nut-Free

Melt the chocolate in the microwave in 30-second intervals, or in a saucepan over low heat on the stovetop.

PREP 10 minutes
MAKES about 2 cups

INGREDIENTS
- 1 cup (2 sticks) unsalted butter, at room temperature
- 1 teaspoon vanilla extract
- 2⅔ cups confectioners' sugar
- 8 ounces semisweet chocolate, melted and cooled
  Pinch of kosher salt

INSTRUCTIONS
In a large bowl, using an electric mixer, beat butter and vanilla on medium-high speed until smooth and creamy, about 1 minute. Slowly add the confectioners' sugar and beat on low speed until fluffy. Add the melted chocolate and salt and beat until just combined, 1 minute. Don't overmix.

Cream Cheese Frosting
Easy • Family Favorite • Nut-Free

It's not just for carrot cake—its tangy-sweet flavor is also delicious on spice or red velvet cake, or try in place of custard in a French-style fruit tart. And cream cheese's texture makes it very easy to work with.

PREP 10 minutes
MAKES about 2 cups

INGREDIENTS
- 1 (8-ounce) package cream cheese, at room temperature
- 6 tablespoons unsalted butter, at room temperature
- 1 teaspoon vanilla extract
  Pinch of kosher salt
- 2 cups confectioners' sugar

INSTRUCTIONS
In a large bowl, using an electric mixer, beat cream cheese, butter, vanilla and salt together on medium-high speed until light and fluffy, about 2 minutes. Add half the sugar and beat on low speed until combined. Add the remaining sugar and beat until smooth.

Brown Sugar-Cream Cheese Frosting
Easy • Nut-Free

Try this take on classic cream cheese frosting by swapping confectioners' sugar with light brown sugar—the taste is reminiscent of cookie dough, so it's a great option for spiced or less-sweet cakes.

PREP 10 minutes
MAKES about 2 cups

INGREDIENTS
- 1 (8-ounce) package cream cheese, at room temperature
- 6 tablespoons unsalted butter, at room temperature
- 1 cup firmly packed light brown sugar
  Pinch of kosher salt

INSTRUCTIONS
In a large bowl, using an electric mixer, beat cream cheese, butter, sugar and salt together on medium-high speed until smooth, about 2 minutes.

Vanilla Frosting

Easy • Family Favorite • Nut-Free

Nothing beats a simple vanilla frosting! Enjoy it as is, or you can customize it by adding extracts or other flavorings to enhance your cakes and cupcakes.

PREP 5 minutes
MAKES about 4 cups

INGREDIENTS

- 1 cup (2 sticks) unsalted butter, at room temperature
- 1 teaspoon vanilla extract
  Pinch of kosher salt
- 6 cups confectioners' sugar, plus more as needed
- ⅓ to ½ cup whole milk

INSTRUCTIONS

In a large bowl, using an electric mixer, beat butter, vanilla and salt together on medium-high speed until smooth, about 1 minute. Add half the sugar and ⅓ cup milk and beat on low speed until combined. Add the remaining sugar, 1 cup at a time, adding more milk, 1 tablespoon at a time, if needed, and beat until smooth. Increase the speed to medium and beat until light and fluffy, about 3 minutes. You can add more sugar and/or milk, if needed, until desired consistency is achieved.

Orange Frosting

Follow Vanilla Frosting recipe, but replace milk with ⅓ to ½ cup freshly squeezed orange juice and add 1 tablespoon freshly grated orange zest (from about 1 orange) when beating the butter.

Peppermint Frosting

Follow Vanilla Frosting recipe, but add ½ to 1 teaspoon peppermint extract when beating the butter.

Whipped Cream Frosting

Easy • Family Favorite • Nut-Free

This classic whipped cream frosting with a sweet kick is perfect for topping off winter-themed treats, such as the Black Forest Cupcakes (page 104) and Hot Cocoa Cupcakes (page 107).

PREP 10 minutes
MAKES about 2 cups

INGREDIENTS

- 1½ cups cold heavy cream
- 1 teaspoon vanilla extract
- ¼ cup confectioners' sugar

INSTRUCTIONS

In a medium bowl, using an electric mixer (or in the bowl of a stand mixer fitted with a whisk attachment), beat cream, vanilla and confectioners' sugar on low speed until slightly thickened, 1 to 2 minutes. Increase speed to medium-high and beat until cream holds soft peaks, 3 to 4 minutes.

Royal Icing

Family Favorite • Nut-Free

This classic icing is perfect for decorating holiday sugar cookies. The meringue powder creates a sturdy icing that hardens quickly.

PREP 10 minutes
MAKES about 3 cups

INGREDIENTS

- 4 cups confectioners' sugar
- 3 tablespoons meringue powder
- ½ cup warm water, plus more as needed
- ½ teaspoon vanilla extract (optional)
  Gel food coloring (optional)

INSTRUCTIONS

1. In a large bowl, using an electric mixer, beat sugar, meringue powder, ½ cup water and vanilla (if using) on medium speed until very thick but still pourable, 7 to 8 minutes. If icing is too thick to drizzle, add more warm water, 1 teaspoon at a time, using a rubber spatula, until desired consistency is achieved.
2. If making colored icing, divide icing among small bowls, one bowl for each color. Add food coloring, a few drops at a time, and stir with a spoon or rubber spatula until desired color is achieved. Cover bowls with plastic wrap until ready to use.

Brown-Butter Glaze

Easy • Nut-Free

This simple recipe is perfect for the Gingerbread Bundt Cake (page 80).

PREP 10 minutes
MAKES about 1 cup

INGREDIENTS

- 4 tablespoons (½ stick) unsalted butter
- 1 cup confectioners' sugar
- 2 tablespoons whole milk, plus more as needed
- ½ teaspoon vanilla extract

INSTRUCTIONS

1. In small saucepan over medium-high heat, melt the butter. Continue cooking until butter is light brown and starting to foam, swirling the pan occasionally. Be careful not to burn. Remove from the heat and let cool slightly.
2. Place sugar in a small bowl or glass measuring cup. Add melted butter, milk and vanilla and whisk to combine. The glaze should be thick but pourable. If needed, add more milk, 1 teaspoon at a time, until it reaches the desired consistency.

5-Minute Icing
Easy • Family Favorite

Many types of flavored extracts work well with this quick and versatile glaze. Adjust the amount of confectioners' sugar and/or milk to achieve the consistency you desire.

PREP 5 minutes
MAKES about 1 cup

INGREDIENTS
- 1½ cups confectioners' sugar
- 3 tablespoons milk or water, plus more as needed for desired consistency
- 1 teaspoon vanilla extract

INSTRUCTIONS
In a glass measuring cup, stir together confectioners' sugar and milk or water until sugar has dissolved. If icing hardens while you are decorating, add more milk or water to soften it.

5-Minute Almond Icing
Replace vanilla extract with 1 teaspoon almond extract.

5-Minute Coconut Icing
Replace vanilla extract with 1 teaspoon coconut extract.

5-Minute Lemon Icing
Replace vanilla extract with 1 teaspoon lemon extract.

5-Minute Mint Icing
Replace vanilla extract with 1 teaspoon peppermint extract.

5-Minute Orange Icing
Replace vanilla extract with 1 teaspoon orange extract.

White Chocolate Filling

Easy • Nut-Free

This luscious filling resembles a chocolate ganache in texture. Once chilled, it's perfect inside Chocolate Sandwich Cookies (page 45).

PREP 15 minutes
CHILL 1 hour
MAKES about 1½ cups

INGREDIENTS

- 12 ounces white chocolate, chopped
- ½ cup heavy cream
  Pinch of kosher salt

INSTRUCTIONS

Place chocolate in a medium bowl. In a small saucepan over medium-high heat, bring cream to a boil. Remove from heat and pour over chocolate. Let sit 5 minutes, then stir with rubber spatula until smooth. Add salt and stir to combine. Cover bowl with plastic wrap and refrigerate until spreadable, about 1 hour.

Peanut Butter Filling

Easy • Family Favorite

This very spreadable mix of butter and peanut butter is delicious as a filling for peanut butter and chocolate sandwich cookies or chocolate cupcakes.

PREP 5 minutes
MAKES about 1 cup

INGREDIENTS

- 4 tablespoons (½ stick) unsalted butter, at room temperature
- ½ cup creamy peanut butter
- 1 cup confectioners' sugar
- 3 tablespoons whole milk
  Pinch of kosher salt

INSTRUCTIONS

In a medium bowl, using an electric mixer, beat butter and peanut butter on medium speed until combined, 1 minute. Add confectioners' sugar and beat until combined, 1 minute. Add milk and salt and beat until smooth, 30 seconds. The filling should be smooth and spreadable, slightly thinner than frosting but not runny.

Cream Filling

Easy • Nut-Free

Combining two fats—here we use shortening and butter—give a recipe the best qualities of both: Shortening makes the filling sturdy, so it won't melt and get all runny. And butter's flavor can't be matched.

PREP 5 minutes
MAKES about 1 cup

INGREDIENTS

- ½ cup (1 stick) unsalted butter, at room temperature
- ½ cup vegetable shortening, such as Crisco
- 1 teaspoon vanilla extract
  Pinch of kosher salt
- 3½ cups confectioners' sugar

INSTRUCTIONS

In a large bowl, beat butter, shortening, vanilla and salt together until well combined. Add confectioners' sugar, 1 cup at a time, and beat on low speed until light and fluffy, about 2 minutes. Add more sugar, if needed, until desired consistency is achieved. (It should hold its shape when spread.)

Peppermint Filling

Follow Cream Filling recipe but substitute 1 teaspoon peppermint extract for the vanilla extract.

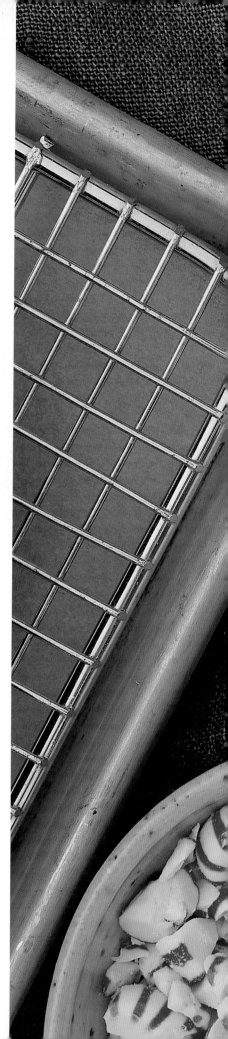

Chocolate Ganache
Easy • Family Favorite • Nut-Free

Easier to make than it looks, this smooth, rich chocolate topping makes every cake droolworthy.

PREP 15 minutes
MAKES about 1 cup

INGREDIENTS
- 8 ounces semisweet chocolate, chopped
- ½ cup heavy cream
- ¼ teaspoon salt

INSTRUCTIONS
Place chocolate in a medium bowl. In a small saucepan over medium-high heat, bring cream to a boil. Remove from heat and pour over chocolate. Let sit 5 minutes, then stir with rubber spatula until smooth. Add salt and stir to combine. Let cool slightly (about 5 minutes) before using.

Recipe Index

Photographer **Nico Oved**   Food Stylist **Amanda Anselmino**

CHOCOLATE
GINGERBREAD
CAKE, PAGE 79

CENTENNIAL BOOKS

An Imprint of
Centennial Media, LLC
1111 Brickell Avenue, 10th Floor
Miami, FL 33131, U.S.A.

CENTENNIAL BOOKS is a trademark of Centennial Media, LLC

ISBN 978-1-951274-90-0

Distributed by
Simon & Schuster, Inc.
1230 Avenue of the Americas
New York, NY 10020, U.S.A.

For information about custom editions, special sales and premium and corporate purchases,
please contact Centennial Media at contact@centennialmedia.com.

Manufactured in China

© 2021 by Centennial Media, LLC

10 9 8 7 6 5 4 3 2

Publishers & Co-Founders Ben Harris, Sebastian Raatz
Editorial Director Annabel Vered
Creative Director Jessica Power
Executive Editor Janet Giovanelli
Design Director Martin Elfers
Features Editor Alyssa Shaffer
Deputy Editors Ron Kelly, Amy Miller Kravetz, Anne Marie O'Connor
Managing Editor Lisa Chambers
Senior Art Directors Lan Yin Bachelis, Pino Impastato
Art Directors Olga Jakim, Alberto Diaz, Jaclyn Loney, Natali Suasnavas, Joseph Ulatowski
Production Designer Peter Niceberg
Copy/Production Patty Carroll, Angela Taormina
Senior Photo Editor Jenny Veiga
Production Manager Paul Rodina
Production Assistants Tiana Schippa, Alyssa Swiderski
Editorial Assistants Michael Foster, Alexis Rotnicki
Sales & Marketing Jeremy Nurnberg